In the Kitchen with
GARY CORCORAN
Recipes from Home and Away

GARY G. CORCORAN

Tellwell Talent
www.tellwell.ca

ISBN
978-0-2288-4543-0 (Paperback)

Table of Contents

Welcome to my kitchen!

My love for cooking started when I was 12 or 13 years old. I come from a big family of ten brothers and sisters. My mother cooked most of the meals at that time, however some of my older sisters occasionally cooked when they were around. Supper, as we always called it, revolved around seven or eight different meals. Getting tired of the same old stuff from week to week, I said to my mother one evening, "Why don't we have pizza for supper one night?" She looked at me and said, "If you want pizza for supper, then make it." So she gave me a pizza kit in a box and I made our first pizza. The box said to add things you liked so I remember pilling on chunks of bologna. It was a hit. The second thing I made was coconut macaroons following a recipe from my mother's Cream of the West (a flour company) cookbook.

My first long-term stint at cooking took place when I went to university. I shared an apartment with three other roommates. We took turns cooking and cleaning. Whoever cooked didn't have to clean up the dishes. Well, the thing I hated most was washing dishes—especially washing dishes after we had a can of beans for supper. I had enough. So I made a deal with my roommates that I would cook supper every night as long as they cleaned the dishes. Thus, my love of cooking began. I bought a couple of cookbooks and started making French dishes first, then curries, stews and so much more.

Over the past 40 years or so, my love for cooking expanded to be more experimental and I got into making charcuterie and different kinds of sausage and smoked meats. I also became confident enough to auction off my talents for charity and have done dinners for ten people with six-course meals and wine pairings. You will see some of those recipes included in this book.

All this to say, cooking for me is not a chore, it is my passion. My wife calls it my obsession. Before I got sick, I would spend many of my Sundays experimenting and cooking the day away. Today I still cook, but it is more about instructing and encouraging others to try my recipes or try new things. I still spend the weekends in the kitchen—now my wife manages the preparation and together we make wonderful dishes that we enjoy together or with friends.

I encourage you to visit my website, www.corcorancooks.com, for more tips and recipes.

Tips from my kitchen

After you have read through some of the recipes in this cookbook, you should notice that I like to use two ingredients: fish sauce and cayenne powder. The purpose of both is to add more flavour to your dish. You shouldn't actually know that either of them are there: you just notice that for some strange reason, your food tastes better. We already know that our taste buds can readily taste sweet, sour, bitter and salty. Fish sauce adds a fifth taste, which is commonly referred to as "umami" or sometimes referenced as savoury. Dried mushroom powder can sometimes provide that umami taste, as well.

In its simplest form, fish sauce is nothing more than fish and salt that has been fermented for anywhere from a few months to a few years. In its purest form, in my opinion, it's freshly caught black anchovies and salt packed into huge wooden barrels and fermented for about 12 months. The natural bacteria breaks down the anchovies producing a briny, fishy umami flavour bomb that knocks the flavours of your finished dish to another level. I use the Red Boat brand because it's one of the best fish sauces made. There are only two ingredients: black anchovies and salt. Many other brands use all kinds of seafood, sugar, artificial colouring, artificial flavours and of course salt. Red Boat is more expensive but worth the extra money. A bottle goes a long way. Many of my recipes call for a teaspoon or more, but start with a few drops first. Taste before and after and you will be amazed as much as I have been. Red Boat fish sauce is easy to find online.

As for cayenne powder, I find adding just a dash to a dish really heightens the flavour. Don't add enough to know it's there, just a dash to get everybody dancing at the party.

Over the years as I read recipes, I quickly discarded many of them because I didn't have an ingredient or two the recipe called for. But as time went on, I learned that a recipe is nothing more than how one person created a dish. You can easily replace one or more ingredients and, yes, your dish may taste different but so what? Who knows, maybe your dish will taste better! Feel free to adjust any of my recipes here. Add or take away any of the ingredients to make it your own.

The chapter on canning and curing or charcuterie contains just a few of the ideas I have experimented with. Once you make your own bacon, you will be so overwhelmed with your results that you may never buy bacon again. You have to make bacon at least once in your lifetime. Even making your own sausages, you know exactly what you are eating.

If you do try your hand at any of the sausages, make sure you buy pink curing salt. It's known by many names, such as Prague powder, instacure, and cure #1. Don't get pink Himalayan salt confused with pink curing salt. Pink Himalayan salt is just salt. Pink curing salt is a mixture of regular salt and sodium nitrite. The sodium nitrite is very important in the prevention of bacteria growth, most notably botulism. Bacteria such as botulism grow in a low oxygen, low acid, moist and warm environment. That's the exact environment we create when we slow smoke sausages, and cure hams and bacon. The sodium nitrite prevents such bacteria from growing.

One last note: all the cooking temperatures referenced in this book are in degrees Farenheit.

Dedication and Thanks

This cookbook would not be possible without all the help I have received. To start, my loving wife Gayle has been at my side in more ways than one. Not only is she working full time, she has been my main caregiver since I was diagnosed with ALS in 2018. She has read all my recipes for errors and has written many of the stories that go with the recipes. She is also my official photographer.

My sister Shirley, my main baker, has made all of my dessert recipes and a number of others, as well. She also took many of the pictures. My brother Bud, who couldn't be with me due to COVID-19, has made many of my recipes from his home in Alberta, and his wife, Anne, photographed the dishes he made. My sister Yvonne experimented with some of my recipes and, last but not least, my sons Colin and Christopher worked on some of the recipes, as well.

A special thanks to my many friends who took time to test some of the dishes and take pictures to include in this book. It truly does take a village to create something like this, including my ultimate cheerleader and supporter, Pauline.

As I pulled this cookbook together, I realized that editing was going to play a big factor in how it was presented and thus I engaged my wife's long-time friend, colleague and our wedding singer, Lynn Patterson, to help us edit the book and provide initial formatting. What is amazing about this is that Lynn was diagnosed with stage IV lung cancer two months after I was diagnosed with ALS. We are both fighting the good fight and this would not read the way it does without her help. Thank you, Lynn.

Appetizers and Finger Foods

Escargot-Stuffed Mushrooms

I have made this dish for both fancy dinners and large summer parties. It's a great appetizer or can be served with other hors d'oeuvres like the prosciutto-wrapped shrimp. The stuffed mushrooms are relatively easy to prepare and can be made ahead of time and stored in the fridge up to 24 hours prior to being baked and served.

Makes: approximately 36
Preheat oven: 450 degrees

INGREDIENTS:

1 can escargots, rinsed
36 small to medium-size mushrooms,
   cleaned, stems removed
1 stick butter (room temperature)
2 shallots, very finely chopped (2T)
2 large cloves garlic, very finely chopped (2T)
1 t dried parsley

1 T brandy, sherry or port
Pinch of cayenne powder
¼ t salt
¼ t fresh ground black pepper
¼ cup Parmigiano Reggiano
   cheese, finely grated

Add softened butter to glass bowl. Mash butter with a fork. (If not soft enough, microwave for a few seconds, but do not melt.) Add remaining ingredients, except the cheese, and mix together.

Add a little butter mixture to each mushroom cap, then add an escargot and top with remaining butter. Sprinkle cheese over each stuffed mushroom.

Bake in a preheated 450 degree oven for 12 - 15 minutes. Pass as finger food before dinner.

Coquilles Saint Jacques

I am lucky to know a scallop fisherman; not only do I get fresh scallops right out of the ocean but he saves me the scallop shells, too. So I get to serve my Coquilles Saint Jacques in the same shells the scallops lived in. If you have never had this dish before, you have to try it. Frozen scallops will work well, too. Make sure you remove the muscle attached to the side of the scallops. It's very rubbery but will add flavour to your stock.

Serves: 4

INGREDIENTS:

1 lb. fresh sea scallops (muscles removed from the side of the scallops and reserved)
4 scallop shells or small gratin dishes for plating

STOCK INGREDIENTS:

½ cup white wine
½ cup clam juice or chicken stock
3 bay leaves
½ t sea salt

A dash or two of cayenne powder
1 clove of garlic, peeled and smashed
    with the side of a knife
Reserved muscles removed from the scallops

In a saucepan, add white wine, clam juice, bay leaves, salt, cayenne powder, smashed garlic clove and reserved muscles removed from the scallops. Bring to a boil and reduce to a simmer, uncovered, for about 5 minutes. Using a slotted spoon, remove and discard bay leaves, garlic and muscles.

Bring your stock back to a boil and add your scallops. Poach on medium heat uncovered for about 3 - 4 minutes for large scallops, or a minute or two for small scallops. Remove from heat. Again using your slotted spoon, remove scallops to a plate. Reduce stock to about half a cup and set aside till you make your béchamel sauce.

INGREDIENTS FOR THE BÉCHAMEL SAUCE:

1 stick butter, halved
½ lb. button mushrooms, sliced
4 large shallots, peeled and finely chopped
3 T flour
½ t sea salt
½ t fresh ground black pepper

½ t fish sauce (optional)
A dash or two of cayenne powder
1 cup whole milk
1 cup grated Gruyère cheese plus a
    little extra to sprinkle on top

In a heavy-bottom pot on medium-high heat, melt half your butter and sauté sliced mushrooms till browned. Remove mushrooms to the plate with your scallops. Now add remaining butter and sauté your shallots till soft, about 5 minutes.

Reduce heat to medium and add flour, salt and pepper, stirring constantly for about a minute. Now add your fish sauce and cayenne powder. Slowly add in reserved stock and milk, stirring constantly till thickened. Stir in cheese and let cook for a couple of minutes.

Preheat broiler to high. Set rack to about 6 inches below broiler.

Divide your mushrooms, scallops and béchamel sauce into four equal portions. Lay out one layer of sliced mushrooms and one layer of scallops to each scallop shell or small gratin dish. Spoon about a quarter of the béchamel sauce atop the scallops in each shell. Top with a little grated cheese.

Place shells on a baking sheet and broil for 3 - 4 minutes till browned and bubbling. If your shells are not sitting flat, lightly crush foil wrap and place scallop shells atop foil before broiling. Remove from oven and rest for a minute, then serve.

Peppercorn Brandy Pâté

Over the years I have sampled a lot of pâté and although much of it was wonderful, in my opinion, nothing comes close to mine. This is a rich, spreadable pâté that I either bottle in small Mason jars or put in ramekins if it is going to be consumed right away. I have often been asked for this recipe and for many years I would not share it. But, as with all good things in life, you should never keep them to yourself, so I am passing this recipe along for everyone to enjoy.

Makes: 18 - 20, 125 ml jars

This recipe takes time, so I've suggested enough ingredients that you can make a large batch for bottling. This recipe yields 18 - 20, 125 ml jars. Once sealed, they will last about 3 months, or more if kept refrigerated.

INGREDIENTS:

1 lb. butter, cut in half
3 lb. chicken livers, picked over to
    remove green bile pieces
4 lb. onions, peeled and chopped
7 anchovies, finely chopped (½ of a 50 g can)
1 cup capers
2 cups red wine

3 t salt
2 t fresh ground black pepper
¼ t cayenne powder
¼ cup brandy
½ cup whole green peppercorns, drained
    (these come in a can or jar packed in water)

Heat a large Dutch oven on medium-high heat. Melt the first half a pound of butter and let brown slightly. Add liver and cook for 10 - 12 minutes, stirring occasionally until slightly browned. Remove liver to a bowl.

Add the second half a pound of butter, add onions and cook for 10 - 12 minutes until onions are partially caramelized. Add remaining ingredients except the brandy and the green peppercorns. These will be added later.

Cook for about 15 minutes until the wine reduces by half. Using an emulsion blender, process the livers until a smooth texture is achieved. (Or you could also process in smaller batches using a food processor until you get a smooth texture.) Stir in brandy and green peppercorns. Keep warm on lowest setting.

Prepare 2 dozen 125 ml Mason jars. (You may not use them all. It totally depends on how much you fill the jars.) Wash jars and lids. Put jars on a cookie sheet and place in 200 degree F oven for 20 minutes. Cover lids with water. Bring to a boil and turn burner to low; keep on low while you start filling the jars.

Remove 3 jars at a time from oven. Spoon pâté into jar, reserving about a ½-inch headspace. Remove 3 lids from the boiling water and place atop jars. Screw lid down tight with a metal band. Tap each jar gently on a folded towel to remove any air bubbles and flatten top.

As jars cool down, they should create a vacuum seal. You should hear them pop. Check the lids. They should be sucked down. Any that have a springy top have not sealed and will not keep longer than a week.

When you are ready to enjoy, slice a baguette in ¼-inch slices. Brush with olive oil. Bake in a preheated 400 degree oven for 4 - 5 minutes. Serve with pâté.

I hope you love this version of pâté as much as I do.

Honey Garlic Chicken Wings

The most difficult part of this recipe is separating the chicken wings. After that, mix everything together and pop in the oven. Pass as finger food while watching your favourite game.

Preheat oven: 325 degrees

INGREDIENTS:

2 lb. of chicken wings
½ cup honey
3 T boiling water
5 large cloves garlic, finely chopped
1 T Heinz 57 sauce or ketchup

1 T Tabasco sauce or your favourite hot sauce
1 T soy sauce
1 t fine sea salt
1 T onion powder

Separate chicken wings into 3 pieces. Reserve wing tips for chicken stock. Place wings in a bowl. Add boiling water to honey in a cup and stir until incorporated. Pour over chicken wings. Add remaining ingredients and stir to coat wings.

Line a sheet pan with foil or parchment paper for easier clean-up. Bake in preheated oven for about 35 - 40 minutes, stirring occasionally till wings are cooked.

Note: If you wish, add all your ingredients to a ziplock bag and refrigerate overnight or for 24 hours. Then bake as outlined above. This will allow you to develop more flavour and a tastier chicken wing.

Shrimp and Scallops in a Garlic Cream Sauce

This is great as an appetizer on its own or added to your favourite pasta as a main course. If you're going the pasta route, add a second cup of cream and stir your al dente pasta into your dish before plating, and leave out the pastry.

Serves: 8

INGREDIENTS:

8 *vol au vent* shells or 8 squares puff pastry
1 lb. raw shrimp, peeled and
    deveined (shells reserved)
1 lb. sea scallops
½ cup butter
4 shallots, peeled and finely chopped
3 large cloves garlic, finely chopped
¼ cup flour
⅛ t cayenne powder

2 t sea salt
½ t white pepper
2 cups white wine
5 bay leaves
1 t dried thyme
1 T fish sauce
1 cup heavy cream (35%)
½ cup Gruyère cheese, shredded

Bake 8 *vol au vent* shells or 8 small squares of puff pastry according to package instructions and set aside.

Remove the stomach muscle attached to the side of the scallops. Set aside to add with the shrimp shells.

In small saucepan, add shrimp shells and the muscle removed from the scallops, along with the white wine and bay leaves. Bring to a boil and reduce to a simmer for a few minutes. Turn off heat and let shells poach in the white wine. Set aside.

Heat a medium-size Dutch oven on medium heat. Add butter and sauté shallots till soft, about 4 - 5 minutes. Add garlic and sauté for another minute. Add flour and cayenne powder, salt and white pepper and stir till flour is incorporated into the butter and shallot mixture.

Strain shrimp-flavoured wine stock into flour mixture and stir to incorporate. Discard shells and bay leaves. Add thyme, fish sauce and stir in heavy cream. Let sauce come to a boil, then reduce to a simmer. Add shrimp and scallops and cook till sauce comes back to a simmer. Cook for another minute or two. Remove from heat and stir in the cheese.

Place a *vol au vent* shell in the bottom of your bowl. Top with the shrimp and scallops along with your garlic cream sauce.

Seared Sea Scallops on Yellow Pea Purée with Salt Riblets and Brown Butter Sauce

I first made this dish to serve when my wife's work colleagues from Toronto came to visit the island for the first time. I wanted them to have a taste of Newfoundland in a simple dish. It received wonderful accolades, so I am passing it along in the hopes you will enjoy it with special friends and family. It does take time to make and requires a pudding bag, but the effort is worth the results. The recipe has its roots in the pease pudding and salt riblets that form part of a regular Sunday dinner in Newfoundland.

Serves: 4

INGREDIENTS:

2 lb. salt riblets or salt ribs
    (see recipe on page 176)
½ lb. yellow split peas
1 onion, peeled left whole
Fresh ground pepper
Pinch of cayenne
2 T butter

¼ cup chicken stock
1 lb. fresh sea scallops (muscle removed)
4 T olive oil
Salt and fresh ground black pepper
½ cup butter
Microgreens to dress your plate

Soak the riblets in water for 24 hours.

Once your riblets have soaked, cover them with cold water, add onion and bring to a boil. Meanwhile, wash peas, place in pudding bag and add to pot with pork and simmer for 3 hours.

Remove pork from pot. Break apart, saving the meat and discarding all fat and bones. Then finely mince and set aside. Squeeze all water from pease pudding while still in the bag.

Remove from bag, add black pepper, cayenne, butter and chicken stock. Mix in reserved minced pork, set aside and keep warm while you prepare the scallops.

Preheat a heavy-bottom fry pan, add oil till shimmering and sear seasoned scallops about 2 minutes per side depending on size. Add a little salt and pepper to taste.

Now make your brown butter sauce. Heat butter on medium heat till deep brown colour achieved, about 4 -5 minutes. You are essentially toasting the milk solids in the butter. Be careful, as it's easy to burn the sauce.

To prepare plate, use a large spoon to spread about 3 - 4 tablespoons of pea purée in 6-inch by 2-inch strips. This will form a bed for the scallops. Place 3 - 4 of the seared scallops along each strip of pea purée. Pour a couple of good tablespoons of brown butter over scallops. Top with a few microgreens for colour.

Serve and enjoy.

Note: If you want to serve this as a main, add some sautéed broccoli rabe with a little fresh garlic and roasted red peppers. My friends Anthony Scilipoti and his wife Ana have made it with fresh green peas puréed in a food processor, avoiding the dried yellow pea process.

Grilled Shrimp with Passion Fruit Sauce

On one of my vacations in Costa Rica, I ordered a shrimp dish with passion fruit sauce. Up to that point in my life I had never eaten passion fruit. The dish was wonderful: sweet, tangy, spicy and fruity, all at the same time. Passion fruit is one of the only fruits that is not picked off a tree, but grows on a vine. A passion fruit is only ripe to eat when it falls to the ground. The fruit is then picked up and used. Here is my take on this wonderful shrimp dish.

Serves: 4
Preheat BBQ: 400 degrees

INGREDIENTS:
1 lb. shrimp, peeled and deveined

MARINADE FOR THE SHRIMP:

¼ cup of honey

2 T fresh lime juice

½ t sesame oil

2 T olive oil

1 t salt

½ t fresh ground black pepper

⅛ t cayenne powder

2 cloves garlic, finely chopped

Whisk together all ingredients for the marinade. Add shrimp and stir to cover. Let marinate for 30 minutes refrigerated. While the shrimp are marinating, make your sauce to serve with the grilled shrimp.

FOR THE SAUCE:

½ cup cold water

6 passion fruits or ½ cup of passion fruit purée

¼ cup rice wine vinegar

¼ cup light brown sugar

1 t fish sauce

⅛ t cayenne powder

Cut the passion fruit in half and scrape out the pulp. Add the pulp and water to a blender and blend on low for about 10 seconds. Strain the purée and discard the seeds.

In a small saucepan add the purée, vinegar, sugar, fish sauce and cayenne. Bring to a boil over medium-high heat. Reduce the heat and simmer until the sauce thickens and is reduced by half, about 15 minutes. Set aside to cool.

Remove shrimp from marinade. Discard the marinade. Spray a little oil on grill. Grill shrimp on direct heat for about 1 minute per side depending on the size.

Pass the shrimp as finger food with the sauce on the side for dipping. Or, to serve as an appetizer, spoon the sauce onto a plate and serve the shrimp atop the sauce.

Prosciutto-Wrapped Shrimp in Garlic Butter

This is a great appetizer or can be served as hors d'oeuvres with other selections like the escargot-stuffed mushrooms.

INGREDIENTS:

1 lb. U16 shrimp, peeled and deveined (U16 means approx. 16 shrimp per lb.)

8 slices prosciutto (sliced in half lengthwise)

8 t Dijon mustard

Dash of cayenne powder

A few drops of fish sauce (optional)

1 stick of butter

4 cloves garlic, crushed

Mix the cayenne and fish sauce into the mustard. Lay out the half piece strip of prosciutto and spread about half a teaspoon of the mustard on the prosciutto. Lay shrimp on one end of the prosciutto and start rolling to cover most of the shrimp.

The goal here is to wrap the shrimp in the prosciutto. The first few generally look bad but you will get better as you go.

Heat butter and garlic in a frying pan on medium-low heat for about 5 minutes to infuse the butter with the garlic. Discard garlic. Increase heat to medium- high and sauté shrimp about 1½ - 2 minutes per side.

Serve and enjoy.

Caesar Salad My Way

Those of you who know me, know I love to cook. Over the years, I've put myself on the block for various charities to be auctioned off to cook a five to six course dinner. After the end of an auction one evening, the lady who was the successful bidder came to me. She asked if I would be willing to serve a Caesar salad for the first course. I knew I would need to make an outstanding Caesar salad, given the money she spent on the dinner. This salad is not your typical Caesar salad. Here it is.

Serves: 4
Preheat oven: 300 degrees

INGREDIENTS:

1 head of romaine lettuce
1 baguette (the fatter version)
2 cloves garlic, peeled and left whole

8 oz. slab bacon or ½ lb. thick-cut bacon, cut into ½-in. pieces
½ cup Parmigiano-Reggiano cheese, shaved

Separate the leaves of lettuce from the head. Keeping them whole, wash and dry them. Set aside.

Cut baguette into 1-inch thick slices. Take out the soft bread in the centre of the baguette leaving nothing but the bread crust ring. This ring of bread is meant to replace your croutons. Bake for 10 - 12 minutes till your rings are crispy. Remove from oven and rub a clove of garlic on cut sides of your bread rings.

If using slab bacon, cut in ¼-inch slices. Then cut the slices into ¼-inch lardons or matchsticks. Add bacon to a cold frying pan. Cook bacon on medium heat for about 10 minutes till crispy. Remove bacon to a paper-lined bowl and keep warm.

DRESSING INGREDIENTS:

2 cloves garlic, finely chopped
2 T lemon juice
1 T Dijon mustard
2 t anchovy paste
1 t Worcestershire sauce

Salt and fresh ground black pepper to taste
Dash of cayenne powder
1 cup mayonnaise
½ cup Parmigiano-Reggiano, fresh grated
Shaved Parmigiano-Reggiano to finish plate

Whisk together the first 7 ingredients in a bowl. When well incorporated, stir in the mayonnaise. Mix well. Add grated Parmigiano-Reggiano cheese and mix well. Set aside.

Now it's time to plate. Take a few leaves of lettuce and sporadically spread a little dressing on each leaf. Gently push the leaves through a bread ring, as if you're inserting a napkin into a napkin ring, being careful not to break the ring. Your bread ring should sit in the middle of the leaves.

Do the same with your other bread rings. Lay the lettuce and bread ring on your salad plate. Drizzle a little more dressing on the lettuce and plate. Top with bacon and a little shaved Parmigiano-Reggiano.

Spinach Salad with Warm Potatoes and Chicken (Livers)

This is a great dish to enjoy whether you like chicken livers or not. I love them but if you don't, replace them with a boneless chicken breast, cut into small pieces. The flavours are still wonderful and it is an easy dish to enjoy during the week or after a busy Saturday or Sunday.

Serves: 2

INGREDIENTS:

2 cups fresh spinach (or more)

8 oz. fresh chicken livers

2 medium potatoes, peeled and thinly sliced

2 - 3 T olive oil

Salt and fresh ground black pepper

Heat a non-stick pan on medium heat. Add olive oil and cook potatoes in a single layer in batches till browned and tender. Add a little salt and pepper. Remove from pan and keep warm.

Add chicken livers to the same pan, adding a little extra olive oil if needed and cook for 8 - 10 minutes till cooked to your liking. Add a little salt and pepper. Remove from pan. Keep warm.

TO SERVE:

Plate spinach, top with warm potatoes and chicken livers. Spoon a couple tablespoons of vinaigrette overtop.

VINAIGRETTE INGREDIENTS:

6 T olive oil

2 T balsamic vinegar

Pinch or two of salt and fresh ground black pepper

Add olive oil, balsamic vinegar, salt and pepper to a Mason jar with lid. Shake for a few seconds till mixed well. Yields about ½ cup.

Salt Cod Bruschetta

A few years ago, our branch hosted the Atlantic Region Summer Educational Conference of Dominion Securities. I created this salt cod recipe to give the Atlantic Canadians and the Come from Aways (CFAs) a taste of Newfoundland in a single bite.

Preheat oven: 400 degrees

INGREDIENTS:

1 lb. dried salt cod
½ cup butter
6 large onions, peeled and finely chopped
1 cup pitted black olives, chopped
½ cup capers, chopped

Fresh ground black pepper
12 oz. goat's cheese, crumbled
6 whole cloves garlic
¼ cup olive oil
1 fresh baguette

Place salt cod in a bowl. Cover with cold water. Change water twice more in a 24 hour period. Place watered cod in a pot. Cover with water and bring to a boil.

Reduce heat and simmer for about 15 minutes. Strain cod, remove skin and bones and discard. Gently break apart cod and set aside. This step can easily be done a day or two in advance.

Peel and finely chop onions. Add butter to sauté pan and sauté on medium heat, stirring often for about 25 - 30 minutes till onions are soft, browned and caramelized. Remove to a bowl and set aside.

To make crostini, choose a good baguette. Slice thinly on the bias. Place sliced bread on a rimmed cookie sheet. Brush top side with olive oil.

Bake in a preheated 400 degree oven for 4 - 5 minutes till slightly firm. Remove from sheet pan and set aside.

Carefully mix cod, caramelized onions, chopped black olives and chopped capers without breaking up fish too much. Add a little fresh ground black pepper and stir in.

Preheat broiler to high. Set rack about 6 inches below broiler.

Rub crostini with fresh peeled whole garlic. Place a tablespoon of cod mixture atop crostini. Top with a little crumbled goat's cheese. Place assembled crostini on sheet pan. Place under broiler for a few minutes to melt goat's cheese.

Pass as finger food before supper.

Open-Face Broiled Scallop Sandwich

This recipe makes a great sandwich but can also serve as a hot hors d'oeuvre. It's a little bulky but tastes delicious. I promise you won't have leftovers.

INGREDIENTS:

1 French baguette
¾ cup garlic mayonnaise (see
   recipe on page 270)
3 T olive oil

1 lb. sea scallops
Salt and fresh ground black pepper
1 cup Gruyère cheese, freshly grated

Slice baguette in half lengthwise. Depending on how many scallops you have and their size, scoop out a little of the centre of the baguette. The goal is to create a pocket for each scallop with a space between them.

Next, spread your garlic mayonnaise along the length of the baguette, being generous in the pockets you created. If using as sandwiches, cut baguette to desired length. Place prepared baguette on a rimmed baking sheet. Set aside your baguette while you prepare the scallops.

Preheat broiler to high. Set rack to about 6 inches below broiler.

Heat oil in a fry pan on medium-high heat. Dry scallops on paper towels. If your scallops are large, cut them in half. Depending on the size, sear them quickly on medium-high heat for a minute or two each side. Add a little salt and fresh ground black pepper. They may not be fully cooked at this stage but they will cook further under the broiler.

Stuff a scallop into each pocket. Put a little fresh grated Gruyère cheese atop each scallop and broil till browned, about 3 - 4 minutes.

If serving as an hors d'oeuvre, cut between each scallop and serve.

Gravlax

Gravlax is a Scandinavian delicacy. It's their way to cure salmon. For this recipe I only use salt, sugar, dill and screech to cure the salmon.

INGREDIENTS:

1 side of fresh Atlantic salmon
(between 3 - 4 lb.)
6 T fine sea salt
1 T fresh ground black pepper

3 T light brown sugar
2 - 3 bunches of fresh dill, coarsely chopped
¼ cup Newfoundland Screech (or use
your favourite vodka or gin)

Place a layer of film wrap on sheet pan. Mix salt, pepper and sugar together. Shake about ⅓ of the mix on the cling film and a little of the dill. Lay salmon skin side down on cling film. Shake balance of mix on flesh side of salmon. Spread dill all over and spoon Screech atop dill mixture.

Fold plastic wrap back up over salmon very tightly. Lay another slightly smaller pan on top with a couple of cans of food to lightly add weight atop the salmon. Refrigerate for 12 hours. Then turn salmon over to allow flesh side to sit in marinade and refrigerate for a second 12-hour period.

After 24 hours, preferably 36 hours, remove from marinade, gently scrape away dill and pat dry. Your salmon is fully cured at this point and ready to eat.

There may be small pieces of dill or black pepper on the salmon. Don't worry. It's part of the curing process and only adds flavour.

Serve immediately or reserve for upwards of 2 days in refrigerator before enjoying. Slice long thin slices on the bias.

Serve with a caper mayo or a mustard sauce on crispy crostini.

Beet-Cured Gravlax

This is a spectacular showpiece and for those who enjoy gravlax, it's delicious to boot. The purple colour of the beets that stain the outer flesh in contrast to the pink salmon inside is a beauty to behold. This is a two-step process and will take a couple of days to make. It creates a beautifully coloured, cured salmon that will impress anyone you serve it to, so it's well worth the time.

STEP 1
INGREDIENTS:

2 beets, washed and quartered

24 juniper berries

Zest of 1 orange

Zest of 2 lemons

2 T light brown sugar

2 T fine sea salt

1 side of fresh Atlantic salmon (3 - 4 lb.)

To make your beet paste, pulverize all ingredients except the salmon in a food processor till smooth. Set aside.

Line a sheet pan with plastic wrap and lay salmon on plastic wrap skin side down. Cover with beet paste. Pull plastic wrap up over salmon. Lay another pan slightly smaller on top with a couple of cans of food to lightly add weight atop the salmon. Refrigerate for 12 hours or overnight.

The next day, scrape away the beet paste. Pat dry with paper towel. Don't worry if there are some little bits of paste left, it will only add to the flavour you are trying to create. Now, move to step 2, and let cure for an additional 24 hours.

STEP 2
INGREDIENTS:

4 T fine sea salt

1 T fresh ground black pepper

1 T light brown sugar

2 bunches fresh dill, coarsely chopped

¼ cup Newfoundland Screech (or
        your favourite vodka or gin)

Place a layer of film wrap on sheet pan. Mix salt, pepper and brown sugar together. Shake about ⅓ of the mix on the plastic wrap along with a little of the dill. Lay salmon skin side down on cling film. Shake balance of mix on flesh side of salmon. Spread dill all over and spoon Screech atop dill mixture. Fold plastic wrap back up over salmon very tightly and refrigerate for 12 hours. After the first 12 hours, turn salmon skin side up to allow flesh side to sit in the marinade, and refrigerate for another 12 hours.

When the second 12-hour marinating period is done, remove salmon from marinade, gently scrape away dill and pat dry. Don't worry if there is a little dill remaining, it will only add to the flavour.

Serve immediately or reserve for upwards of 2 days in refrigerator before enjoying. Slice long thin slices on the bias. Serve with a caper mayo on crispy crostini. Enjoy.

Stuffed Mussels

Fresh mussels may be difficult to find. Look at the mussels before you buy them to ensure most of them are closed. If a lot of them are gaping open, don't buy them as they are probably not fresh and many may be dead.

Preheat oven: 425 degrees

INGREDIENTS:

5 - 6 dozen fresh large mussels (about 4 lb.)
½ cup white wine
7 bay leaves

BREAD CRUMB STUFFING:

1 stick butter
1 large onion, finely chopped
6 mushrooms, finely chopped
4 cloves garlic, finely chopped
1 t fish sauce (optional)
1 t fresh chopped thyme

¼ t cayenne
½ cup fresh parsley, chopped
2 cups fresh breadcrumbs
½ cup Gruyère cheese, grated
¼ t salt
½ t fresh ground pepper

Heat butter in medium-size Dutch oven till it starts to brown. Add onion and mushrooms and sauté till soft and tender, about 8 - 10 minutes. Add garlic and cook for a couple more minutes. Stir in fish sauce if using.

Remove from heat and stir in remaining ingredients. There should be enough butter to help the ingredients stick together; if not, add a little mussel stock till all ingredients stick together. Set aside till mussels are prepared.

PREPARE MUSSELS:

Aggressively wash the mussels in several changes of cold water. Start by adding your mussels to a bowl or in your sink and half cover with cold water. Get both your hands in and aggressively move the mussels around, rubbing the shells together. Your water should look murky at this time. Rinse and repeat till water is clear.

Now it's time to pick over the mussels. Any that are open may be dead and should be discarded. To check if the mussel is dead or alive, give the shell a tap against a hard object. If it's alive, it will slowly start to close, so it's good to keep. If it's doesn't close, discard it.

The opposite is also true once the mussels are cooked. Any mussels that remain closed after cooking should be discarded as they are dead. Don't attempt to open them, just discard immediately. Only use the mussels that have opened wide.

In pot large enough to hold your mussels, heat on high for a minute. Add wine, bay leaves and mussels. Cover and cook for about 7 - 8 minutes till mussels have opened and partially disconnected from their shells.

Discard any mussels that are still tightly closed. They are dead and should not be consumed. Remove one shell and disconnect mussel if still attached to the other shell. Place mussel back in the shell ready to be stuffed. Place all mussels on a rimmed cookie sheet. Continue with remaining mussels.

Once all mussels are prepared, top with a couple teaspoons of stuffing depending on the size of the mussel. Bake in oven for 10 minutes to heat through. Pass as finger food.

Seafood Dip

This seafood dip is a simple dish to make and also delicious if you like seafood. It's best made a day in advance to let the flavours develop. Lay out at cocktail hour and let people serve themselves.

INGREDIENTS:

8 oz. package cream cheese at
    room temperature
2 t hot sauce
½ t fresh garlic, very finely chopped
1 t sea salt
½ t fresh ground black pepper
1 T onion powder

½ cup mayonnaise
1 t Worcestershire sauce
1 T seafood sauce or ketchup
2 T chicken stock
2 cups of your favourite fresh cooked
    seafood, finely chopped

Mix together all ingredients except the seafood. Stir till well mixed. Fold in seafood. Spoon into a serving dish.

Serve with thinly sliced baguette or your favourite crackers.

Foie Gras Terrine

I first experimented with foie gras about 30 years ago. I searched through my cookbooks but couldn't find a recipe. Those were the days before the internet. Over the years I made notes—and made mistakes—and this is the culmination of my efforts. I know it's good because my friend JP's mother who is very French told me it was the best foie gras she had ever eaten. If you have never tried foie gras before, this recipe is for you.

INGREDIENTS:

2 lobes foie gras at room temperature
    (about 1 lb. each)
3 cups whole milk
1 T fine sea salt
¼ t pink curing salt (optional)
1 t sugar

1 t white pepper
1 cup Sauternes
Truffles, if desired
Boiling water
You'll also need a piece of board or
    cardboard to compress the terrine.

The first step is to remove the veins from the foie gras. Taking your time, pull apart the lobe using a sharp knife, gently following the veins and remove them. Continue pulling the lobe apart and hook the tip of your knife under the veins. Try to pull them out without breaking them.

Continue following the veins, all the while separating the lobe. Don't worry if the lobe is coming apart. You won't notice it in the final dish. Work until you have removed as many veins as you can find.

Now work on the second lobe. Once completed, place lobes in glass dish and cover with whole milk. Gently massage the lobes to try and remove the blood stains. Cover dish with plastic wrap and place in the refrigerator for an hour.

Remove from refrigerator and gently massage the lobes again where you pulled the veins to help remove more of the bloodstains. Cover and refrigerate overnight. You know you have done a good job if milk has turned completely pink.

The next day, drain and rinse the lobes in cold water and pat dry completely with paper towel. Place dried foie gras in a glass dish and pour ½ cup of Sauternes over the foie gras. Massage the Sauternes into the foie gras. Let marinate refrigerated for a few hours.

Now it's time to make your terrine.

Remove foie gras from refrigerator and drain Sauternes (reserve for another use). Mix salts, sugar and pepper. Sprinkle on all sides of your foie gras, ensuring to cover all sides, and use all the salt and pepper mixture. It may seem like a lot but it truly is required to flavour the terrine.

Using remaining ½ cup of Sauternes, pour a little in bottom of terrine; place a large piece on the bottom, smooth side down.

Now layer truffles (if using) and any small pieces of foie gras. Next, fit in the balance of foie gras, smooth side facing up to form a smooth top. Gently press down foie gras to fill the terrine. Pour balance of Sauternes over foie gras and shake any leftover salt mixture from the bowl on top. Cover terrine.

Place terrine in a baking dish almost the same height as the terrine. Pour boiling water in the baking dish to at least half the height of the terrine. Bake, covered in preheated oven at 200 degrees F for approximately 30 - 40 minutes. Check the internal temperature after 30 minutes. The temperature should read between 90 and 100 degrees F maximum. If so, remove from the oven.

There should be a small amount of fat starting to show around edges.

Pour off excess fat and reserve. Let terrine cool for an hour at room temperature. Cut a board slightly smaller than the terrine, cover with cling film and place atop the terrine. Place a weight on the board to help compress the terrine.

Refrigerate overnight. The next day, remove terrine from refrigerator, warm the reserved fat and pour over the terrine to help fill in sides of pan and form a thin layer of fat on top of the terrine. Allow terrine to firm up in the refrigerator for an hour or so.

When ready to serve, run a warm knife around the inside of the terrine. Invert terrine onto a cutting board or platter. Reinvert terrine back again. Using a warm knife, cut into ½-inch slices.

Plate with sliced apples sautéed in Calvados and toasted brioche bread. Serve with a glass of Canadian ice wine or a glass of Sauternes.

Wild Rabbit Terrine

I made this terrine for one of my charity dinners. You will note that I have included "wild" in the title as there is a big difference between wild and farm-raised rabbit. I never buy farm-raised rabbit in the stores. If you can't get your hands on wild rabbit, go ahead and use the farm-raised stuff, albeit it won't be as good, in my opinion.

Preheat oven: 325 degrees

INGREDIENTS:

1 cup whole pistachios, shelled
2 wild rabbits
2 lb. fatty pork belly or shoulder cut into strips
½ lb. beef suet (optional)
1 medium onion, cut in quarters

1 T fresh thyme leaves
1 T fine sea salt
1 t fresh ground black pepper
½ cup whole green peppercorns
1 lb. thin-sliced bacon

Cover pistachios with boiling water and let sit for 1 hour. Remove as much of the skin as possible. Drain and set aside.

Debone the rabbits. Reserve bones for stock. If you wish, you can add the liver and heart to be ground with the remaining rabbit. I always do. Be extra careful when removing the loins from the back. They will be used whole in the centre of your terrine. You will have 4 loins.

Now it's time to grind your meats. If your pork belly or shoulder is very lean, replace about half a pound with beef suet. Cut your pork belly in strips. Add deboned rabbit, except the loins, and pass through the coarse grinding plate of your grinder. Grind your onion, rabbit liver, heart and suet, if using, along with the meats to incorporate well. Collect your grindings in a big bowl or pan large enough to hold all your ingredients.

Add drained whole pistachios, fresh thyme leaves, salt, fresh ground black pepper and green peppercorns. Using your hands, gently mix all ingredients together until well combined.

Prepare your terrine, which is a deep, rectangular, straight-sided dish (usually ceramic, glass or cast iron) with a tight-fitting lid. If yours doesn't have a lid, wrap it in a double layer of foil tightly wrapped around when baking. The one I use is about 12 in. x 4 in. x 4 in.

Start by laying the bacon slices crossways in your terrine. The bacon should be overhanging the sides of your terrine. Cut a couple of pieces of bacon to cover both ends.

Now half-fill your terrine with your ground rabbit mixture. Press down to ensure it is packed tight, especially in the corners. Lay your loins side by side down the middle. You should have two loins running the full length of your terrine.

Now cover the loins with the remaining mixture. You may have leftovers depending on the size of your terrine. Fold the overhanging bacon back over the top.

Place cover on your terrine and put in a deep baking dish half-filled with hot water. Transfer to oven and cook for 1½ to 2 hours. Check internal temperature after 1½ hours by inserting thermometer into the centre of terrine. You are looking for 150 degrees F.

Remove from oven, uncover and let cool for up to an hour. Cut a board or a double layer of cardboard slightly smaller than the terrine, cover with cling film and place atop the terrine. Place a weight on the board to help compress the terrine. Refrigerate overnight.

When ready to serve, place terrine in a hot water bath for a few minutes, then invert your terrine onto a serving board. Slice, and serve with pan-seared peach slices, baby gherkins, green salad and toast points.

Octopus Terrine

My friend JP once gave me an octopus, and I promised him I would cook it for us to enjoy together. This is the recipe I created. We had so much fun plating it that we ate it all and forgot to take pictures. Oh well!

INGREDIENTS:

One 3 - 4 lb. octopus (beak removed)
½ cup sea salt
5 - 6 onions, peeled and cut in half
2 carrots, coarsely chopped
2 celery stalks, coarsely chopped
½ cup black peppercorns, crushed

13 bay leaves
2 gelatin leaves
Black olive tapenade, pulverized to
    a liquid (optional garnish)
You'll also need a piece of board or
    cardboard to compress the terrine.

In a large pot, place octopus in pot and cover with 2 - 3 inches of cold water. Remove octopus from water and set aside. Add the sea salt, chopped vegetables, peppercorns and bay leaves. Bring pot to a boil, then reduce to medium heat to help develop flavour for about 30 minutes.

Increase heat to bring your stock back to a boil. Now dip octopus 3 times slowly in your pot of boiling stock. Then drop the octopus in and simmer for 40 minutes to 1 hour till tender. Cool octopus in an ice bath. Remove the octopus arms (tentacles) and reserve. Use body for another recipe.

NEXT:

Take 1 cup of the octopus-poaching liquid, add 2 gelatin leaves or enough gelatin powder to the liquid to set according to package instructions. Stir till melted. Line terrine with plastic wrap.

PACK IN TERRINE:

Add ½ cup of gelatinized broth to terrine. Firmly pack tentacles tight. Add more broth to cover if necessary. Reserve any gelatinized broth. Cut a piece of board or cardboard the size of the terrine. Wrap in plastic wrap. Place atop of terrine and lay a couple of cans of food to weight down, then chill.

Let set overnight with weight on top. Next day, remove weight, heat reserved gelatinized broth and pour a little on top to ensure octopus is fully covered. Chill again.

Next day, invert terrine on cutting board. Cut into ¼ - ½ inch slices.

PLATING:

Overlap 3 thin slices on a serving plate and drizzle a little olive oil over the octopus. Add a few flakes of fleur de sel. Decorate with a few drops of pureed black olive tapenade.

Finish decorating the plate by adding fresh ground black pepper, some julienned slices of dried tomatoes packed in oil, grated slices of Parmigiano-Reggiano, toasted pine nuts or some micro greens. You can even add some deep-fried capers, dried first on paper towel. Serve.

Smoked Pork Rillettes

Rillettes are another one of France's delicacies. It's a French preservative technique much like a confit. For this one, I have used heavy smoked bacon and pork hocks along with pork shoulder. The meats are then seasoned and slow cooked in pork or duck fat on low heat for hours. Then, the meats are shredded and packed into a terrine. I like to serve them like I do a patê, along with a warmed sliced baguette, while having drinks before dinner.

INGREDIENTS:

3 whole fresh pork hocks (approx. 2.7 kg)
2 lb. pork shoulder, cut into 1-in. cubes
600 g heavy smoked bacon (about 2
    ½ cups), cut into small pieces
1 T salt
1 t fresh ground black pepper
⅛ t cayenne powder

1 T fish sauce
1 cup white wine
½ cup water
7 bay leaves
4 - 5 cups pork fat (lard) or duck fat
1 cup carrots, peeled and cut into ¼ -in. dice

Pack all the meats and the balance of ingredients except carrots into a heavy-bottom pot. Melt enough pork fat or a combination of pork fat and duck fat to cover all the meats. Cut a circle of parchment paper slightly smaller than your pot and place on top to cover meats. Cover and bring to a simmer for 2 hours. Add carrots and continue simmering for another 2 hours on very low heat. Remove from heat.

When cool enough to handle, remove meats from pot. Discard bay leaves. Remove all meat from the bones, discarding all skin and bones. Chop all meat into small pieces. Keep warm. Try and keep the carrots as intact as possible and set aside.

Remove as much fat from the stock while still warm, reserving both. At this point, we will use all the stock. It's going to be very rich and gelatinous. Bring the stock back to a boil. Turn off heat. Add chopped meats back to the stock.

In true French tradition, there is a lot of the fat added back to the meats. However, I only add about a ½ cup of the reserved fat to the meats. Stir in the ½ cup of fat to incorporate it into the meats. Add back the carrots.

You want the temperature of your pot to be at 125 degrees F before you add the rillettes to your terrine. Either slowly increase the heat or let it cool to allow the temperature to reach 125 degrees F. This will ensure the added fat stays incorporated in the meats.

Spoon rillettes into your terrine or small ramekins and let cool.

Enjoy with a warmed sliced baguette.

Note: Terrines will last for up to a week refrigerated and longer if you pour a thin layer of fat on top.

Pork and Chicken Rillettes

If you have never had rillettes, you are in for a treat. This is another one of France's delicacies. Rillettes are a French preservative technique much like a confit. Various meats are seasoned and then slow cooked in fat for hours. The meats are then shredded and packed into a terrine. I serve them like I do a pâté, along with a sliced baguette, while having drinks before dinner.

INGREDIENTS:

6 whole chicken legs
1 full pork hock
1 cup white wine
1 T white pepper
4 t sea salt

⅛ t cayenne
1 t fish sauce
1 cup onion, finely chopped
4 - 5 cups pork fat (lard) or duck fat
1 cup carrots, peeled and cut into ¼-in. dice

Pack all the chicken legs and pork hock and the balance of ingredients except carrots into a heavy-bottom pot. Melt enough pork fat or a combination of pork fat and duck fat to cover all the meats. Cut a circle of parchment paper slightly smaller than the size of the pot and place on top to cover meats. Cover and bring to a simmer for 2 hours. Add carrots and continue simmering for another 2 hours on very low heat. Remove from heat.

When cool enough to handle, remove chicken and pork from pot. Remove all meat from the bones, discarding all skin and bones. Chop all meat into small pieces. Keep warm. Try and keep the carrots as intact as possible and set aside.

Remove as much fat from the stock while still warm, reserving both. At this point, we will use all the stock. It's going to be very rich and gelatinous. Bring the stock back to a boil. Turn off heat. Add chopped meats back to the stock.

In true French tradition, there is a lot of fat added back to the meats. However, I only add about a ½ cup of the reserved fat to the meats. Stir in the ½ cup of fat to incorporate it into the meats. Add back the carrots.

You want the temperature of your pot to be at 125 degrees F before you add the rillettes to your terrine. Either slowly increase the heat or let it cool to allow the temperature to reach 125 degrees F. This will ensure the added fat stays incorporated in the meats.

Spoon rillettes into your terrine or small ramekins and let cool. Enjoy with warmed baguettes.

Note: Terrines will last up to a week refrigerated. They will last longer if you pour a thin layer of fat on top.

Crab Cakes

I find the issue with most crab cakes is that they contain more bread or potatoes than actual crab, and that's exactly why I normally hesitate to order them in restaurants. The shellfish really shine through in my crab-heavy recipe below.

Yields: about 12 crab cakes depending on how big you make them

INGREDIENTS:

1 ½ lb. fresh crabmeat
4 T butter
4 large shallots or 1 medium
    onion, finely chopped
1 red bell pepper, finely chopped
3 cloves garlic, finely chopped
125 ml bottle capers, drained, chopped

¼ t cayenne powder
2 t Old Bay seasoning
Salt and fresh ground black pepper to taste
½ cup breadcrumbs
¾ cup mayonnaise
1 t fish sauce

BREADING MIXTURE:

2 eggs, beaten
2 cups breadcrumbs

Fresh ground black pepper

Start by picking through the crab to ensure there are no pieces of cartilage.

In a sauté pan, melt butter on medium heat. Sauté onions 4 - 5 minutes. Add bell pepper, garlic and capers. Continue to sauté another 4 - 5 minutes.

Move pan ingredients to a medium-size bowl. Add cayenne powder, Old Bay seasoning, a little salt and fresh ground black pepper and breadcrumbs. Mix together.

Place bowl in refrigerator to cool for about 15 minutes.

Remove from refrigerator and stir in the mayonnaise and fish sauce. Gently fold in the crabmeat, being careful not to break it up too much.

In a shallow bowl, beat eggs. Put the breadcrumbs in a second shallow bowl. Add a little fresh ground black pepper and stir.

Now it's time to make the crab cakes. You should have enough mixture to make a dozen crab cakes about 2.5 inches in diameter.

If you're going to serve them as hors d'oeuvres, make them half that size. Make the cakes one at a time, dip in the beaten egg and roll in breadcrumbs. Place the cakes in refrigerator for 15 - 20 minutes to firm up.

Heat a sauté pan on medium heat. Add a little olive oil and sauté the cakes 3 - 4 minutes per side. I like to serve mine with a chipotle mayo sauce: simply chop a couple of canned chipotle peppers and stir into a cup of mayonnaise.

Cod au Gratin

This is a classic Newfoundland dish, great for cold winter nights or cool, rainy summer days. Many people say that fish and cheese don't go together, but I can guarantee this dish will change your mind. I always recommend using fresh cod, but I have often used frozen cod for this dish, especially in the winter, when there are few options.

Serves: 8
Preheat oven: 425 degrees
Cook time: 20 minutes

INGREDIENTS:

3 cups fresh milk
3 lb. fresh cod, cut into large chunks
2 t salt
¾ cup butter
2 large onions, peeled and finely chopped
¾ cup flour
Dash of cayenne pepper

½ cup white wine
1 t fish sauce
2 T chicken bouillon
Fresh ground pepper
2 cups cheddar cheese (grated and divided)
1 cup fresh breadcrumbs
¼ cup olive oil to drizzle over breadcrumbs

In a medium pot, warm milk, add cod and salt, and simmer on low heat for 5 minutes.

Meanwhile in a large pot, melt butter and add chopped onions. Cook on medium-low heat for about 10 minutes until onions are opaque but not browned. Stir in flour and cayenne and cook for a couple of minutes. Add white wine, fish sauce and bouillon.

Remove fish from your pot and add the remaining heated milk in small amounts to your onions and butter, stirring constantly until all the milk is absorbed and sauce becomes thick. Add fresh ground pepper to taste.

Cook on very low heat for 3 - 4 minutes; add 1½ cups of the grated cheddar and stir until incorporated.

Move some of the larger chunks of cod to your shallow ovenproof dish, or individual ramekins if using. Add remaining cod to your cheese sauce and gently stir in. Remove from heat and spoon over cod in your shallow ovenproof dish or individual heatproof ramekins.

Mix remaining ½ cup of grated cheddar to breadcrumbs with the fresh ground pepper and sprinkle atop cod. Pour a light drizzle of olive oil over breadcrumbs.

Bake in a preheated 425 degree oven for about 20 minutes or until bubbling and the breadcrumbs are golden brown. Reduce cooking time by 5 minutes if you're using individual ramekins.

Remove from the oven, let cool for 5 minutes and serve.

Crab au Gratin

Fresh crab may be difficult to get your hands on. Frozen is okay but your dish will not be as good.

Serves: 4

INGREDIENTS:

1 lb. fresh crabmeat (remove cartilage)
½ cup butter
2 small onions, finely chopped
1 clove garlic, finely chopped
½ cup flour
½ t dry mustard
⅛ t cayenne powder
½ cup white wine

2 T chicken bouillon
1 T fish sauce
3 bay leaves
1½ cups milk
½ t salt
½ t fresh ground white pepper
1 cup mild cheddar cheese
¼ t paprika

On medium-low heat, using a heavy-bottom pot, melt butter and add chopped onions; cook for about 10 minutes until onions are cooked but not browned, just opaque. Add garlic and cook for another minute or so. Stir in flour, dry mustard and cayenne and cook for a couple of minutes. Add white wine, bouillon, fish sauce and bay leaves.

Let cook for a couple of minutes. Add warmed milk in small amounts, stirring constantly till all milk is absorbed and sauce becomes thick. Add salt and fresh ground white pepper to taste.

Cook on very low heat for 3 - 4 minutes, add cheese and stir till melted. Add crabmeat and gently stir in. Remove from heat. Discard bay leaves.

Preheat broiler. Move rack to 6 inches below broiler.

Place in prepared crab shells or small ramekins. Top with a little paprika.

Broil for 3 - 4 minutes till bubbling. Serve and enjoy.

Lobster au Gratin

This is a delicious and rich mixture of lobster cheese and butter. I would recommend serving this in smaller portions because dinner size is really too much. It is a wonderful way to use up leftovers from the large feed of lobster you had the previous night.

Serves: 6
Preheat oven: 375 degrees

INGREDIENTS:

2 cups fresh milk
1 lb. fresh cooked lobster meat,
     cut into small pieces
½ cup butter
3 medium onions, peeled and finely chopped
3 cloves garlic, finely chopped
½ cup flour
Dash of cayenne pepper
½ cup white wine
1 t fish sauce

2 T chicken bouillon
Fresh ground white pepper
½ cup Gruyère cheese, grated
½ cup Parmigiano-Reggiano, grated
2 russet potatoes, peeled and very thinly sliced
1 t sea salt
½ cup cheddar cheese, grated
1 cup fresh breadcrumbs
¼ cup olive oil to drizzle over breadcrumbs

Melt butter and add chopped onions, cook on medium-low heat for about 10 minutes until onions are cooked but not browned, just opaque. Add garlic and cook for another minute or so.

Stir in flour and cayenne and cook for a couple of minutes. Add white wine, fish sauce and bouillon. Add warmed milk in small amounts, stirring constantly till all milk is absorbed and sauce becomes thick. Add fresh ground white pepper to taste.

Cook on very low heat for 3 - 4 minutes, add Gruyère and Parmigiano-Reggiano; stir till melted. Add lobster meat and gently stir in. Remove from heat. Brush a little melted butter or spray a little vegetable oil over the bottom of your shallow baking dish.

Heat a pan with a couple of cups of water. Bring to a boil and add salt. Blanch sliced potatoes for about 1 minute. Drain and dry. Place sliced potatoes in an overlapping pattern in bottom of your dish.

Now, spoon the lobster over the potatoes. Add your grated cheddar to breadcrumbs with the fresh ground white pepper and sprinkle atop lobster. Pour a light drizzle of olive over breadcrumb mixture.

Bake in oven for about 30 minutes or until dish begins to bubble.

Remove and let cool for about 5 - 10 minutes before you serve.

Pineapple Salsa for Oysters

Nothing packs a punch of the sea like a simple raw oyster, but they can be intimidating for first-time oyster eaters. This is a great salsa that will help novices enjoy their first oyster, and give veterans a new flavour to enjoy.

INGREDIENTS:

2 cups fresh ripe pineapple sliced (you can use canned slices if that's all that's available)
½ cup red pepper, finely chopped
½ cup shallots, finely chopped
1 T chili, finely chopped (use your favourite: mine is Habanero)

1 t fish sauce (optional)
Juice of 1 lime
2 oz. vodka
Salt and pepper to taste

Peel pineapple and cut into slices. Grill pineapple to get some nice grill marks. Remove from grill and finely chop. Add about 2 cups to a medium bowl. Add remaining ingredients to bowl and stir.

Cover and let sit overnight to bring all the flavours together. Prepare raw oysters and spoon ½ teaspoon of salsa on each fresh shucked oyster.

Makes enough salsa for 8 - 10 dozen oysters.

Soups

Beef Stock

Making stock is a chore. So when you are at it, make a lot. Same energy, bigger results. I once made a caribou stock with about 50 pounds of bones. I then turned the stock into about 2 gallons of consommé. And yes, I have a pot big enough to hold 50 pounds of bones and more! All stocks are made without the addition of salt. Since the stock is always reducing, if you add salt it will become very salty. So only add salt at the end or to your finished dish.

Preheat oven: 425 degrees

INGREDIENTS:

5 - 10 pounds of beef bones
5 carrots, chopped
5 celery stalks, chopped
5 onions, chopped
5 cloves garlic crushed
½ cup tomato paste

Drizzle of olive oil
½ cup sherry
1 cup red wine
7 bay leaves
1 T whole black peppercorns

Place chopped vegetables and bones in a large roaster. You don't need to peel the vegetables. Add garlic and stir in tomato paste. Drizzle with a couple of tablespoons of olive oil and roast for about 1 hour to an hour and a half till the bones and vegetables are nicely browned. Stir occasionally.

Remove from oven and place bones and vegetables in large empty pot. Add a little water, sherry and red wine to roasting pan, scraping roaster of all brown bits and adding to pot with bones. Cover bones with cold water, add bay leaves and whole peppercorns and bring to boil.

Reduce heat and simmer uncovered for about 2 hours, stirring and smashing vegetables occasionally. Keep an eye to level of stock, adding a little water if necessary. Using a strainer, strain stock into another pot. You now have a wonderful beef stock.

Note: This stock helps make a delicious French onion soup. It freezes well, too.

Chicken Stock

Making stock is a chore. So when you are at it, make a good batch. I always buy bone-in chicken breasts and bone them myself, freezing the bones for stock later. I cut the tips off the wings and freeze them, too. All stocks are made without the addition of salt. Since the stock is always reducing, if you add salt as you go, it will become very salty. So only add salt at the end.

Preheat oven: 425 degrees

INGREDIENTS:

5 - 6 lb. of chicken bones and wing tips

3 carrots, chopped

3 celery stalks, chopped

3 onions, chopped

Drizzle of olive oil

7 bay leaves

1 T whole black peppercorns

¼ cup vinegar or white wine

Place chopped vegetables and chicken bones in a large roaster. There's no need to peel the vegetables. Drizzle with a couple of tablespoons of olive oil and roast for about 1 - 1½ hours till the bones and vegetables are nicely browned. Stir occasionally.

Remove from oven and place bones and vegetables in large empty pot. Add a little boiling water to roaster, scraping roaster of all brown bits and add to pot with bones.

Cover bones with cold water, add bay leaves, vinegar and whole peppercorns and bring to boil. Reduce heat and simmer uncovered for about 2 hours, stirring and smashing vegetables occasionally. Keep an eye to level of stock, adding a little water if necessary. Using a strainer, strain stock into another pot. You now have a wonderful rich chicken stock.

Note: This stock forms the base of a great chicken soup. I love making chicken soup especially during flu season. It freezes well, too.

Easy Mexican Chicken Soup

Often when you think of chicken soup, it is associated with times of sickness. This is a soup I always made for my wife, Gayle, when she was sick. (Thankfully, I haven't had to make it for her recently.) Gayle is not a fan of meat in her soup, so this is chicken soup without the chicken. Ultimately, it is just a good homemade chicken broth with vegetables, a touch of cumin and a little mozzarella cheese. It's a simple and quick soup.

Serves: 8 (or in Gayle's case: 8 servings over 4 or 5 days of healing)
Preheat oven: 350 degrees

INGREDIENTS:

8 cups chicken stock (preferably homemade)
½ t ground cumin (or to taste)
1 onion, peeled and finely chopped
2 large carrots, peeled and chopped
3 celery stalks, chopped

1 small rutabaga or turnip, peeled and chopped
1 cup mozzarella cheese, shredded
4 small flour tortillas, cut into ½ -in. strips
A few fresh tomatoes (optional)
Salt and fresh ground black pepper

Add chicken stock, cumin and vegetables to a medium-size pot. Bring to a boil, then reduce heat to a simmer.

Simmer for about 25 - 30 minutes till the vegetables are tender. Taste and add salt and fresh ground black pepper to your liking.

Meanwhile, cut tortillas into strips. Place on a cookie sheet and bake till they are dry and crispy, about 7 - 8 minutes.

Dish up your soup, adding a few tortilla strips and top with a little shredded mozzarella cheese. Enjoy.

Note: If you like tomatoes, add a couple of chopped fresh tomatoes about 5 minutes before serving.

Lobster Stock

Any time you have the chance to cook lobster, it's a great time to make lobster stock. But making lobster stock is a chore. If you roast the shells inside, be prepared for a smelly kitchen. My wife, Gayle, doesn't like either the taste or the smell of lobster, so . . . my advice is to roast the shells outside on the BBQ. All stocks are made without the addition of salt. Since the stock is always reducing, if you add salt as you go, it will become very salty. So only add salt at the end. When it comes to the vegetables, don't worry about quantities; the more the merrier.

INGREDIENTS:

Reserved lobster shells
3 carrots, chopped
3 celery stalks, chopped
3 onions, chopped
2 cloves garlic, crushed
3 T tomato paste

Drizzle of olive oil
½ cup sherry
1 cup white wine
7 bay leaves
1 T whole black peppercorns

Preheat oven or BBQ to about 425 degrees. Place chopped vegetables and empty lobster shells including bodies in a roaster. There's no need to peel your vegetables.

Add garlic and stir in tomato paste. Drizzle with a couple of tablespoons of olive oil and roast for about 1 hour, till shells and vegetables are nicely browned. Stir occasionally.

Remove from oven or BBQ and place in large empty pot. Add a little water, sherry and white wine to roasting pan, scraping roaster of all brown bits and add to pot with shells. Cover shells with cold water, add bay leaves and whole peppercorns and bring to boil.

Reduce heat and simmer UNCOVERED for about 1 - 2 hours, smashing shells and vegetables occasionally. Keep an eye to level of stock, adding a little water if necessary. Strain stock into another pot adding reserved liquid from lobster shells when you've removed the lobster from the shells. You now have a wonderful lobster stock.

Note: Use this stock for a delicious lobster bisque or for the base in a gumbo. The stock freezes well, also.

Coq-a-Leekie Soup

Our whole family congregated at my parents' house every Christmas Eve and that's where I first made this chicken and leek soup. I think I cooked three whole chickens in a very large boiler that first year and we made enough soup to feed everyone, about 40 of us in total. Even today, my niece, DJ, with a family of her own, still makes this soup for Christmas Eve. This soup is very popular in Scotland and Wales, where prunes are sometimes added. The leeks, barley and shredded potatoes make this a very thick soup. Here is the recipe in a more manageable size than my first effort.

INGREDIENTS:

1 whole chicken or chicken parts (about 4 - 5 lb.)	1 T sea salt
¼ cup chicken bouillon	1 T fish sauce
2 large carrots, peeled and chopped into chunks	½ t fresh ground black pepper
	1 cup pot barley
3 - 4 large sticks of celery, cut into chunks	2 large onions, peeled and finely chopped
2 large cloves garlic, smashed with the side of your knife	6 large leeks, white parts only
	1 large russet potato, peeled and shredded
7 bay leaves	1 t dried thyme
	1 cup heavy cream (35%), optional

In a pot big enough to hold your chicken, cover with cold water, add chicken bouillon, carrots, celery, garlic, bay leaves, salt and fish sauce, cover and bring to a boil. Reduce heat to a simmer and cook for an hour and a half. Remove chicken from pot to cool. Discard bay leaves, carrots, celery, and garlic. Reserve stock.

When it's cool enough to handle, take the chicken off the bones. Cut into bite-size pieces. Reserve chicken. Discard skin and bones.

While chicken is cooking, prepare your onions and leeks. Don't peel or shred potato till later. To prepare leeks, cut away the tough green leaves and cut off the root section. You only want to use the white part, although some of the light green parts are perfectly good to use. Now split the leek lengthwise. Put leeks under running water to wash away any mud or grit that has collected there. Cut into ¼-inch slices. Set aside.

Bring stock back to a boil. Add pepper, barley, onions and reduce heat. Cook for about 20 minutes. Shred your potato now. Add leeks, shredded potato and thyme. Continue simmering for about 15 minutes. Now add chicken and heavy cream if using. Let simmer till soup is hot. Serve with crusty bread.

Lentil Soup

As the resident family chef, many of my relatives call me for cooking ideas or recipes. One afternoon, my father-law, Wilf, did just that. He wanted to make lentil soup, but found the online recipes too complicated, so he called me for some advice. This isn't something I had made often, but my imagination started going and before I knew it, I had a recipe to send him. Later that week, I tried cooking it for dinner myself. Delicious! You can enjoy this healthy soup on any cold day for lunch or dinner. If you are a vegetarian, replace the chicken stock with vegetable stock.

Serves: 8

INGREDIENTS:

3 T olive oil
2 onions, finely chopped
1 cup carrot, finely chopped
1 cup celery, finely chopped
1 t garlic, finely chopped
2 cups dried green or brown lentils, rinsed
     in several changes of cold water
1 cup chopped tomatoes

8 cups sodium-free chicken broth
1 t fish sauce (optional)
1 t dried thyme
⅛ t cayenne powder
2 t salt
1 t fresh ground black pepper
3 bay leaves

Optional: This is a great time to use up that rind of Parmigiano-Reggiano you have been saving. Use about a ½ cup, cut into ¼-inch dice. If you do use the rind, reduce salt by ½ teaspoon.

Heat a large heavy-bottom pot over medium heat. Add olive oil. Once hot, add the onion, carrot and celery. Cook until the onions are translucent, approximately 7 - 8 minutes. Add garlic and cook for 1 minute.

Now add the remaining ingredients and stir to combine. Increase the heat to high and bring to a boil. Reduce the heat to low, cover and cook on low until the lentils are tender, approximately 45 minutes.

Before serving, check for seasoning and adjust if necessary. Serve with crusty rolls.

Enjoy.

Note: If you prefer a creamier soup, purée using a hand blender, then stir in ½ cup of whipping cream (35%).

Oxtail Soup

Originally, oxtail came from the tail of an ox. Now it describes meat that comes from the tail of cattle of either sex. The oxtail traditionally includes a section of tailbone with some marrow in the centre and a bony portion of meat surrounding the tail. It is full of flavour, and makes a rich-tasting soup.

Serves: 12 - 15

INGREDIENTS:

3 T olive oil
4 - 5 lb. of oxtails
1 large onion, peeled and finely chopped
2 large carrots, peeled, coarsely chopped
3 celery stalks, coarsely chopped
1 clove garlic, very finely chopped
½ cup barley

2 cups red wine
6 cups beef stock
6 cups of water
7 bay leaves
1 T sea salt
2 t fresh ground black pepper

Heat 3 T of olive oil in a heavy pan. Sauté the oxtails on medium-high heat for 10 minutes, turning often until browned. Add onions, celery and carrots. Sauté for 4 - 5 minutes, stirring occasionally. Add garlic and sauté for an additional minute or so. Add barley, wine, stock, water, bay leaves, salt and pepper.

Bring to a boil, then reduce to the lowest setting and simmer for 2 - 2 ½ hours.

Skim any accumulated fat from the surface of your soup. Remove bay leaves and discard. Adjust seasoning.

Serve soup as is or remove oxtails from the soup, let cool and pick the meat from the bones. Add meat back to the soup, discarding bones. Warm soup and serve.

French Onion Soup

I will be honest, I was not going to include French onion soup in my cookbook, as it's commonly found in most recipe books and served at all levels of restaurants. However, I realized this project would not be complete without adding my version. Normally, my goal is to have a variety of seven to eight different types of onions included in my soup. This isn't mandatory, but is a nice differentiator when you are describing your soup as you serve it.

Serves: 8

INGREDIENTS:

6 lb. of onions, any combination of yellow, white, red, sweet, Spanish, pearl, cipollini, shallots and green onions or leeks, peeled and sliced

One stick butter (¼ lb.)

¼ cup brandy

10 cups good beef stock

1 cup port

1 T fish sauce (optional)

1 T Worcestershire sauce

A couple good dashes of cayenne powder

5 bay leaves

Salt and fresh ground black pepper to taste

8 - 10 oz. Gruyère cheese, grated

8 slices of bread cut ½-in. thick from a baguette

Peel and cut onions in half, top to bottom, and slice. Heat a heavy-bottom pot on medium heat and melt the butter. Add onions to pot and stir to cover with the butter to caramelize the onions. This should take between 20 - 30 minutes. Be careful not to burn the onions. Stir often.

You are looking for very soft, light brown onions. When you have reached this stage, add the remaining ingredients except the cheese and the bread. Bring to a boil and immediately reduce heat to a simmer.

Cover and simmer for about 20 minutes to bring all the flavours together. Discard bay leaves.

Turn on the broiler. Place a rack about 6 inches below broiler.

While the soup is simmering, slice the baguette, and pop the slices in a toaster or bake in a hot oven until crispy.

Now, place your bowls on a baking sheet, ladle the soup into each bowl, and top with the toasted bread and about 1 oz. of cheese. Place the baking sheet about 6 inches from the broiler and broil for 2 - 3 minutes until the cheese is melted and bubbling. Be careful not to burn the bread and cheese.

Remove from the oven and let sit a few minutes before serving.

Fire-Roasted Red Pepper Soup with Pears and Stilton

This is not your normal soup. Be prepared for the accolades. Try to enlist some help roasting and peeling the peppers. It is also great to portion off and freeze as a basic roasted red pepper soup (without the pear or Stilton) for future dinners or lunches. If you are a vegetarian, replace the chicken stock with vegetable stock.

Serves: 8

INGREDIENTS:

6 red peppers
1 t olive oil
3 medium onions, finely chopped
1 stick butter (approximately 8 T)
6 T flour
1 t paprika (preferably smoked paprika)
¼ t cayenne pepper
1 cup white wine

6 cups chicken (or vegetable) stock, divided
½ t fish sauce
2 cups fresh or bottled pears, chopped into ½-in. pieces
8 oz. (or more if you like) Stilton cheese, crumbled
Salt and pepper to taste (white pepper, preferably)

To begin, roast whole red peppers, rubbing them with a little olive oil and roast over an open flame, high heat on a BBQ or under a broiler in oven, turning often until skin is completely black.

Remove from heat and put them in a bowl, cover in plastic wrap and set aside for 20 minutes to ½ hour. This allows the peppers to cool and the steam helps the skin to come off easier. (Alternatively, use store-bought roasted red peppers, rinsed very well.)

Meanwhile, sauté onions in butter for about 10 minutes in heavy-bottom stockpot on medium heat, stirring occasionally until onions have softened and started to brown. Add flour, paprika and cayenne to pot and cook for about two minutes stirring constantly without the flour browning. Slowly whisk in the wine followed by 1 cup of chicken stock.

When fully incorporated into the flour and onion mixture, stir in remaining stock and fish sauce. Bring to a light boil, reduce heat and simmer for approximately 10 minutes.

Remove all the black and blistered skin from the red peppers and be sure to remove the seeds and membranes from inside.

DO NOT wash the red peppers with water. Coarsely chop peppers. Add to stockpot along with any juices that have accumulated in the bowl and blend into a creamy soup using a handheld immersion blender.

Otherwise, working in small batches, add to a blender, being careful of hot liquid, and blend to incorporate all ingredients into a smooth, creamy soup. Continue to simmer for another 10 minutes or so. Don't worry if a few tiny bits of black skin stay on the peppers. After all, it's a fire-roasted red pepper soup.

Soup is now ready to be served or can be kept on a very low heat until ready to serve. Likewise, soup can be chilled and reheated on very low heat the next day, stirring occasionally.

To serve, pour about 1 cup of hot soup into each bowl, add ¼ cup of pears and top with the crumbled Stilton.

Fire-Roasted Tomato Bisque
with Herbs and Stilton

For starters, this tomato bisque will be one of the easiest bisques/soups you will ever make. Once you make it a couple of times, you won't need to measure anything. If you have lots of fresh tomatoes on hand, use them and skip the canned tomatoes. Use whatever fresh herbs you have on hand, or dried, and in whatever quantities you like. Use white wine or vegetable stock instead of chicken stock. Skip the flour if you prefer a thinner soup style. Love onions? Add more. Hate onions? Omit them. Like seafood? Add a couple of cups of small pieces of halibut or cod and scallops or shrimp at the end and slowly cook for another few minutes. Add a little saffron and replace the chicken stock with a seafood stock and you have a very easy bouillabaisse. Omit the Stilton if you're making the bouillabaisse. Remember, this is your bisque: make it the way you like it.

Serves: 8
Preparation time: 40 minutes

INGREDIENTS:

2 lb. of fresh plum tomatoes
6 T olive oil
4 T butter
2 small onions, peeled and finely chopped
2 cloves garlic, finely chopped
3 T flour

1 (28 oz.) can, whole tomatoes
   (fire-roasted, if you can find them)
2 cups chicken stock
4 T fresh dill, finely chopped
2 T fresh thyme, finely chopped
Salt and pepper to taste
8 oz. piece Stilton, crumbled

You can make this bisque in about 40 minutes. It's always better the next day, so if you have time, make it the day before and reheat just before serving.

Start by cutting your plum tomatoes in half lengthwise, toss in a bowl with 2 tablespoons of olive oil and roast on a grill. Roast 8 - 10 minutes, turning a couple of times until they get a little charred. Remove from grill. Remove any of the skin you can, then coarsely chop and set aside in a bowl.

Meanwhile, heat a Dutch over on medium heat, melt butter with remaining 4 tablespoons of olive oil and add finely chopped onions and sauté them on medium heat for 6 - 8 minutes until they are soft. Add garlic and sauté for another minute.

Now add flour and cook for about 1 minute; whisk in chicken stock and simmer for about 10 minutes. Coarsely chop canned tomatoes and add to fire-roasted ones. Be sure to add the juice in the can as well. Now add all tomatoes and accumulated juice to pan. Add salt and fresh ground pepper to taste. Chop herbs and add to pan.

Simmer for a few more minutes and serve, or refrigerate and serve the next day. If serving right away, top with a few tablespoons of crumbled Stilton, or add croutons if you prefer.

Lobster Bisque

Lobster bisque is made more from the shells than from the actual lobster meat. It's a slow process but well worth the effort. Plus, you'll still have the lobster meat to use for another dish. If you wish, however, you can finish the bisque with a few pieces of lobster to make it more decadent.

Serves: 8
Preheat oven: 425 degrees

INGREDIENTS:

2 live lobsters (between 1 ½ - 2 lb. each)
1 gallon boiling water (about 20 cups)
½ cup sea salt
3 carrots, chopped
3 medium onions, chopped peel and all

3 celery stalks, chopped
3 T tomato paste
2 cloves garlic, crushed
7 bay leaves
1 T black peppercorns

To boil lobster, bring water to a boil in a large pot and add sea salt. Add lobsters and bring back to a boil for 7 - 8 minutes. Remove lobster to cool. Discard water. Remove lobster from shells, reserving all liquid that drains from shells. You will add this to the finished stock later. Start by removing the big claws and tail. Lay the tail on its side and use the heel of your hand to push down and crack the tail. Remove the meat. Split tail down back to form two even halves, forming the letter C. Remove intestine that runs down the tail.

Using a heavy cleaver, crack claws. Remove meat from shells, then remove the cartilage from the claws. This should yield about 1 pound of delicious lobster meat. Note: Lobster is still in a raw state at this point.

Now place all the shells including the bodies in a roasting pan. Add chopped vegetables and garlic. You don't need to peel the vegetables. Stir in the tomato paste. Roast in preheated oven for about an hour. Browning the shells and the vegetables will add colour and flavour to the bisque.

Place the roasted shells and vegetables in a stockpot. Add the bay leaves and peppercorns. Add 10 cups of boiling water to the roasting pan scraping any brown bits from the pan. (Do not use the water you previously used to cook the lobsters; it's too salty.) Add to stockpot.

Simmer uncovered for at least an hour, preferably two hours. Stir stock occasionally and use a potato masher to mash the shells and vegetables. Strain the stock through a sieve and reserve. Discard the shells and vegetables. Reserve the stock.

MAKE THE BISQUE:
INGREDIENTS:

2 sticks butter
2 onions, finely chopped
½ cup flour
⅛ t cayenne pepper
¼ cup brandy

1 cup white wine
1 t fish sauce (optional)
8 cups of reserved lobster stock
1 cup whipping cream (35%)

In a heavy-bottom pot, melt butter on medium-high heat. Sauté onions till soft. Stir in flour until it is well incorporated. Add cayenne pepper. Stir in brandy, white wine and fish sauce. Add reserved lobster stock and any reserved liquid that came from the lobster when you removed the meat from the shells. Using a hand-immersion blender, purée stock. Add whipping cream. Bring back to a slow simmer.

Serve with or without the reserved lobster. If using the lobster, chop into ½-inch cubes.

Newfoundland Split Pea Soup with Dough Boys (Dumplings)

This soup was a staple in every Newfoundland household in years gone by. By boiling the bone of a ham, a delicious broth was created. Then, by adding a bag of dried split yellow peas, a few vegetables and what we always called dough boys (mainlanders would call these dumplings), you'd have a delicious meal on the cheap. Whenever I baked a ham, I always made a big pot of pea soup afterwards. A few days later, when I was tired of eating the soup, I added a little curry powder to give it a whole new flavour. I hope you try it.

Serves: a dozen hungry mouths

INGREDIENTS:

1 leftover ham bone

15 cups water

7 bay leaves

3 cups dried split yellow peas (washed)
   or whole dried green peas

2 t fresh ground black pepper

1 T fish sauce (optional)

A couple of good dashes of cayenne powder

2 - 3 large onions, peeled and finely chopped

2 large carrots, peeled and diced small

1 small rutabaga or turnip,
   peeled and diced small

4 cups smoked ham, diced

Cut off most of the ham from the bone. Reserve for later. Add the ham bone and bay leaves to a large heavy-bottom pot. Cover with about 15 cups of water and bring to a boil. Cover and reduce heat to a simmer for about 2 hours.

Remove ham bone and discard (or give the bone to your lucky dog, as we would have done). Skim any fat from the surface and discard. Remove and discard bay leaves.

Now add your split peas, pepper, fish sauce, cayenne powder and chopped onions. Simmer for about 40 - 50 minutes, stirring occasionally. Add the diced carrots, rutabaga and diced ham. Continue to simmer for another 10 - 15 minutes.

Meanwhile, prepare mixture for dough boys. Just before you add your dough boys, taste the soup for salt. Add as necessary. Stir your soup well before adding dough boys to make sure the peas are not sticking to the bottom of your pot.

Now add the dough boys to your pot. Cover and continue to simmer for about 15 more minutes. DO NOT REMOVE THE COVER. Serve soup along with the dough boys.

INGREDIENTS FOR THE DOUGH BOYS:

2 cups flour

4 t baking powder

A good pinch of salt

1 stick cold butter, finely chopped

2 eggs, beaten

⅔ cup whole milk

Sift together the flour, baking powder and salt. Stir in chopped butter. Using your fingers, work the butter into the flour. Now stir in the eggs and milk. Stir till just combined. Do not overwork the dough.

Drop the dough into the soup using heaping tablespoons. Cover and simmer for about 15 minutes without taking a peek unless you want soggy dough boys.

Corn Chowder

My love of cooking started very early. I remember being 18 or 19 years old and driving downtown St. John's to visit a kitchen store that had just opened. After browsing for a few minutes and finding a few things I wanted to buy, I noticed they had a little soup-and-sandwich shop at the back of the store. It was there that I had my first taste of corn chowder. I don't think there has been a summer since that I haven't made some version of this chowder.

Serves: 8

INGREDIENTS:

10 ears fresh corn, cleaned and
    kernels cut off the cob
½ lb. sliced bacon, cut into small pieces
2 T butter
2 medium onions, finely chopped
1 large clove of garlic, finely chopped
¼ cup flour
6 cups chicken stock

3 bay leaves
1 T fish sauce
1 t salt
½ t fresh ground black pepper
⅛ t cayenne powder
1 lb. red potatoes, washed, unpeeled
    and cut into ½-in. dice
½ cup heavy cream (35%)

Heat a heavy-bottom pot on medium heat. Immediately add your chopped bacon to your cold pot. Sauté your bacon 8 - 10 minutes till crispy. Remove bacon to a bowl and set aside. Ensure you leave the bacon fat behind.

Add butter and onions. Sauté 6 - 8 minutes till soft. Add garlic and sauté for another minute or so. Stir in the flour and let cook for a minute or two while stirring constantly.

When your flour is incorporated well, gradually add your chicken stock. Then add bay leaves, fish sauce, salt, pepper and cayenne powder, and bring to a boil.

Now add your corn and diced red potatoes. When your pot comes back to a boil, reduce heat to a simmer. Cover and simmer for about 20 minutes till the potatoes are tender. Add cream and bring back to a simmer. Remove and discard bay leaves.

Add reserved bacon bits and serve. Soups and chowders are always best served with crusty bread and this one is no exception.

Note: If you want a slightly thicker soup, use a hand-immersion blender to purée soup for a few seconds until desired consistency is reached. After I have removed the kernels from the cob, I like to scrape the cobs with the back of a chef's knife to remove any small pieces of corn. You will also get some juice from scraping the cobs, which will add more flavour to your chowder.

Delicious Cod Chowder

Cod chowder is a staple in many Newfoundland households. Like most recipes, countless versions abound. Replace the cod with haddock if it's the only fresh fish available. Frozen will do in a pinch, but it won't be as good as fresh.

Serves: 4 - 6

INGREDIENTS:

1 ½ lb. fresh cod or haddock, boneless and skinless
3 T butter
3 onions, peeled and finely chopped
1 carrot, peeled and finely chopped
2 sticks celery, finely chopped or shredded
1 clove garlic, finely chopped
3 T flour

2 large potatoes, peeled and chopped into small pieces
2 cups fish stock or clam juice
2 cups chicken stock
3 bay leaves
2 t sea salt
½ t fresh ground black pepper
Dash or two of cayenne powder
¾ cup whipping cream (35%)

Heat a heavy-bottom pot on medium heat. Melt butter and sauté onions, carrots and celery till somewhat soft, about 10 minutes. Add garlic and sauté for another minute.

Stir in the flour, then gradually add stock and stir till incorporated. Add bay leaves, salt, pepper and cayenne powder.

Next, bring to a boil and add potatoes, then reduce heat to a simmer. Cover and simmer for about 15 minutes till potatoes are tender. Add cod and simmer for another 5 minutes. Don't worry about cutting up the cod, it will easily fall apart when serving.

Add cream and bring back to a simmer. Discard bay leaves and serve along with warm crusty bread.

Note: If you want to turn this into a seafood chowder, simply include a few shrimp and scallops when adding your cod.

71

Crab Bisque

I love crab, but for me it has to be fresh and warm, right out of the shell. However, this is a great way to use crab outside of those perfect conditions.

Serves: 10 - 12

INGREDIENTS:

1 ½ lb. crab, removed from shell
   (snow crab is my preference)
2 sticks butter
2 cups onion, finely chopped
2 cups celery, finely chopped
1 small carrot, finely chopped
½ green pepper, finely chopped
2 cloves fresh garlic, finely chopped
½ cup flour

1 T Old Bay seasoning
¼ t cayenne
4 t fish sauce
7 bay leaves
½ cup white wine
4 cups seafood stock
2 cups chicken stock
1 cup heavy cream (35%)

Melt butter on medium-high heat. Add onion, celery, carrot and green pepper. Sauté vegetables till soft, 10 - 12 minutes. Add garlic, stirring for another 2 minutes. Incorporate flour into vegetables.

Add seasonings. Add white wine and stir to incorporate. Add stock in small amounts all while stirring. Once all the stock is incorporated, reduce heat to a simmer and continue cooking for 30 minutes.

Stir in the heavy cream and bring back to a simmer. Remove and discard bay leaves. Add the crabmeat and stir in gently to get the crab incorporated but without breaking it up.

Serve with crusty bread.

Hearty
One-Pot Dishes

Paradise Chicken Gumbo

I created this recipe for a magazine about 25 years ago: so long ago I don't even recall which magazine it was. I do remember that they provided a list of mandatory ingredients I had to use. This is the recipe I created. It calls for a lot of stirring but it is well worth the effort. Prepare onions, garlic, chicken, tomatoes, mushrooms and peppers before starting to make the roux. This should take about 20 minutes. The total cooking time should be slightly more than one hour. With all the chopping and stirring involved, it is a great dish to involve your guests for casual entertaining.

Serves: 6

INGREDIENTS:

½ cup vegetable oil
¾ cup all-purpose white flour
4 cups onions, coarsely chopped
3 - 4 cloves garlic, crushed
1 Habanero pepper, finely chopped (optional)
3 lb. boneless skinless chicken
    thighs, cut into small pieces
1 ¾ cup low-salt chicken stock
4 sun-dried tomatoes, chopped
    or broken into pieces

1 large portobello mushroom,
    chopped, stem removed
4 large sprigs fresh thyme
1 T sea salt
3 cups green bell peppers, coarsely chopped
1 lb. raw shrimp, peeled and deveined
2 cups green onions
Ground cayenne pepper

RICE

2 ¼ cups water
1 cup long grain rice

¼ t salt

This gumbo starts with a roux. Set a heavy 4-quart cast-iron or other heavy-bottom pot over medium heat. When hot, add oil and heat 3 minutes. Add flour, stirring constantly with a flat-bottom wooden spatula. Stir until combined and slowly turns a light brown colour.

Continue stirring for about 15 - 20 minutes longer or until roux is a chocolate brown colour. Roux has to be stirred continuously to prevent burning. This is an essential step in making a good gumbo.

Increase heat to medium, add chopped onions and garlic, and if you like it hot, add finely chopped Habanero pepper. Stir occasionally for 5 minutes. Add chicken; stir occasionally for 10 minutes. Add chicken stock, sun-dried tomatoes, mushrooms, thyme and salt. Let simmer for additional 15 minutes while stirring occasionally.

While gumbo is simmering, prepare ingredients to make rice by bringing water to a boil. Add rice and salt, stir, cover and reduce heat to lowest setting. Cook without removing cover for 20 minutes. Remove from heat, fluff with fork and keep warm.

Add bell peppers to gumbo and simmer for 10 minutes. Add shrimp and green onions and simmer for additional 5 minutes or until shrimp are just cooked. Remove from heat.

Add ½ cup of rice to bowl and spoon gumbo over top. Pass the cayenne pepper for those with a passion for hot food.

Serve with crusty rolls.

Louisiana Gumbo

Every chef in New Orleans has their own version of gumbo, a full flavoured soup/ stew with a combination of ingredients generally drawn from whatever you have on hand. However, there are a few things that are common to any good gumbo. The first thing is a good roux, followed by a hearty stock of simmered shrimp shells, chicken or pork stock. Then there is the holy trinity: a combination of onions, celery and green peppers. A good gumbo will generally have a combination of meats and seafood which could include chicken, andouille sausage, tasso ham, pork, rabbit, squirrel, shrimp, crawfish, crab and the list continues. You are, in essence, using up what you have in your fridge. See page 182 for my tasso ham recipe.

Now, a roux is basically flour cooked in oil, stirred constantly to cook the flour and eventually brown the flour. The longer you cook the flour, the browner it becomes to the point you can actually burn it. The Cajuns in Louisiana generally cook three different types of roux: blond, brown and dark brown. The darker the roux, the less stock it will absorb. You should have all your vegetables and meats prepared in advance. Once the roux is finished, you want to immediately add your holy trinity: your onions, celery and green peppers.

Gumbo is a project, so when I make it, I make a lot. This one will feed a dozen hungry mouths. Don't be concerned about quantities of vegetables and or the meats. More or less of either won't make a big difference. If you like heat like I do, add more of your favourite hot peppers.

Serves: 10 - 12 hungry mouths

INGREDIENTS:

1 cup vegetable oil
1 cup all-purpose white flour
4 cups onions, coarsely chopped
1 cup celery, coarsely chopped
2 cups green pepper, coarsely chopped
2 lb. pork shoulder, cut into ½-in. pieces
1 lb. andouille sausage or any smoked
    sausage, cut into slices
½ lb. tasso ham or any good ham
    cut into ½-in. pieces
5 cups lobster or chicken stock
7 bay leaves

5 - 6 cloves garlic, crushed
2 t salt
½ t fresh ground black pepper
3 T fresh thyme leaves
1 Habanero pepper, finely chopped (optional)
2 cups red bell peppers, coarsely chopped
1 lb. raw shrimp, peeled and deveined
    (save the shells for your stock)
1 bunch green onions, chopped

In small saucepan, add shrimp shells, chicken stock and bay leaves. Bring to a boil and turn off heat. Let shells poach in chicken broth. (When ready to use, remove and discard shrimp shells and bay leaves). Set aside.

Now it's time to make the roux.

Set a heavy 4-quart cast-iron or other heavy-bottom pot over medium heat. When hot, add oil and heat for 3 minutes. Add flour, stirring constantly with a flat-bottom wooden spatula. Stir until combined and slowly turns a light brown colour.

Continue stirring for about 15 - 20 more minutes or until roux is a chocolate brown colour. Roux has to be stirred continuously to prevent burning. This is essential in making a good gumbo.

Now it's time to build your gumbo. Add the holy trinity (onions, celery and green peppers) and stir to incorporate into the roux. Add the pork shoulder, sausage and ham. Stir and cook for 6 - 8 minutes.

Add stock and stir. You want enough stock to fully cover all ingredients in your pot. Your gumbo will be soupy at this stage. Now stir in the garlic, salt, pepper, thyme and Habanero.

Reduce heat to low and simmer, covered, for 30 - 40 minutes, stirring occasionally. Taste the pork to ensure it's tender. If it's tough, cook a little longer.

With cover removed, add red peppers and cook for 5 - 6 minutes. Add green onions and shrimp, cooking for another 5 - 6 minutes. Taste, adjust seasoning. Serve with pecan rice if you can find it. If not, use your favourite rice.

Note: if you wish you can bake the roux in a 400 degree oven for about 20 minutes but you still need to stir it occasionally.

Chicken Stew

Chicken stew is generally considered a mainstay for cold winter nights. For my family it is a go-to comfort food that we eat after a long day of hard work in the garden or in the office or when we are experiencing periods of sadness or worry. Everyone needs a few recipes that feed their soul, so I hope this one gives you warmth on a cold night or comfort during difficult times.

Serves: 8

INGREDIENTS:

4 T olive oil

3 lb. of chicken, cut into pieces

3 onions, coarsely chopped

2 cloves garlic, chopped

4 T flour

5 sticks celery, chopped

2 large carrots, peeled and chopped

1 small rutabaga or turnip, peeled and chopped

2 large potatoes, peeled and cubed

4 cups chicken stock

½ cup white wine

1 t fish sauce

1 T soy sauce

7 bay leaves

Salt and pepper to taste

In a large heavy pot, heat the olive oil and sauté the chicken. You are only looking to brown the chicken, not cook it. Remove the chicken from the pot.

Sauté the onions until browned, then add the garlic, cooking for another minute or so. Stir in the flour, which will thicken the stew. Add a little more oil if necessary to cook the flour.

Now add the chicken stock, white wine, fish sauce, soy sauce, bay leaves, salt and pepper. Return the chicken to the pot. Now add the vegetables. Simmer for 1 hour or until vegetables are tender. Discard bay leaves.

Serve with crusty rolls.

Note: Consider making the pastry on page 242 for added comfort.

Beef Stew

This is a delicious hearty meal for a cold winter's night. I really love making this in the fall when fresh vegetables are available. Stews like this one are always better warmed up the next day.

Serves: 8

INGREDIENTS:

2 lb. stewing beef, cut into 1-in. cubes
½ cup flour
1 T paprika
2 t salt
2 t fresh ground pepper
⅛ t cayenne
1 large ziplock bag
½ cup olive oil
3 large onions, peeled and chopped
1 large clove garlic, crushed

2 T tomato paste
1 cup red wine
1 t Worcestershire sauce
1 t fish sauce
4 cups good beef stock
2 large carrots
1 large parsnip
2 large potatoes
Small turnip or rutabaga

Add flour and seasonings to ziplock bag. Shake to mix ingredients, then add beef cubes to flour mixture in bag. Shake to cover all the beef cubes with the flour mixture.

Heat oil in heavy-bottom pot; sear beef in batches till browned on all sides. Remove and set aside.

Add onions and garlic and stir to brown for about 5 minutes. Add flour remaining in ziplock shaker bag to onions and stir till well mixed into the onions. Add tomato paste, red wine, Worcestershire sauce and fish sauce. Stir and simmer for a few minutes.

Add beef stock and beef, stir and simmer for about 45 - 50 minutes till beef is almost tender.

While beef is cooking, peel and coarsely chop vegetables. Keep covered in warm water till ready to use.

When beef is almost tender, add vegetables to stew and simmer till tender, about 40 minutes more. Adjust seasoning. Serve with crusty dinner rolls.

Note: Consider making the pastry on page 242 for added comfort.

Wild Rabbit Stew

Wild game is wild. Wow. That was a statement. No, what I mean is that wild game can be unpredictable. It can be cooked in 30 minutes and be wonderful, yet, another time, might need three hours of cooking and still be tough. Many times my mother cooked two or three rabbits in the same pot for supper. After a couple of hours of slow roasting, two might be as tender as hell and one would be as tough as shoe leather. I cooked two Canada geese for a dinner party a few years ago. I started them early afternoon. One was done in a couple of hours. The other one is still in the oven now. (Joking, of course, but it never did get tender enough to serve.) So, my storyline for cooking wild game is like Forrest Gump's box of chocolates. You never know what you are going to get. Some wild game cooks quickly, some doesn't. It really depends on what that wild animal spent the last few hours doing before it became your dinner. So enjoy it for what it is.

I love making stew. It's so comforting. I also think the real beauty of making a stew is that it is very difficult to mess up. Even if you overcook it, it's still wonderful. You can use any wild game here. Rabbit is my favourite wild game but I love partridge, too, and it's my second choice for this stew.

Moose, caribou or black bear would also make this dish delicious. You'll just need to reduce your cooking time if you're using big game meat. Using wild rabbit, it takes close to three full hours to finish baking the dish. Use whatever root vegetables you prefer or have on hand. The pièce de resistance, if you wish, is the baked pastry cooked on top of the stew. Add another 25 minutes baking time if you're including the pastry.

Preheat oven: 350 degrees
Serves: 6 - 8

INGREDIENTS:

¼ cup olive oil
2 wild rabbits, about 5 lb. total (separate the rabbits into 6 pieces each, the 4 legs, the body and the backs)
1 large ziplock bag
½ cup flour
4 large onions, chopped
½ cup brandy

2 cups red wine
4 cups beef stock or water
1 t soy sauce (optional)
1 T fish sauce (optional)
1 T sea salt
1 t fresh ground pepper
7 bay leaves

Add flour to bag, add rabbit and shake to cover. Heat oil in heavy-bottom pan large enough to hold the rabbit and all the vegetables. Sauté rabbit in batches to brown nicely. Remove browned rabbit to a bowl, then add onions and sauté for 5 - 6 minutes.

You may need to add a little more oil. Add remaining flour in shaker bag. Stir till flour is well incorporated into onions. Add back rabbit. Add brandy, stir till almost evaporated. Add remaining ingredients and bring to a simmer. The rabbit should be completely covered in liquid.

Remove from heat, and bake covered in a 350 degree preheated oven for approximately 1½ - 2 hours. Some wild rabbits are much tougher than others, as previously mentioned. Cook till almost tender. Add vegetables and cook another 40 minutes.

FOR THE VEGETABLES:

4 - 6 cups of carrots, turnip, parsnip and potatoes

Peel vegetables, chop coarsely. Keep covered in warm water till required. Add to stew with about 40 - 50 minutes remaining. I am inclined to hold back the parsnip for 10 minutes as it cooks more quickly than most vegetables.

Adjust oven temperature to 375 degrees.

FOR THE PASTRY (IF DESIRED):

2 cups flour, plus a little additional flour for the board
4 t baking powder
2 eggs beaten
⅔ cup cold whole milk
A good pinch of salt
1 stick cold butter, chopped

FOR THE PASTRY:

The key to a good tender pastry is handling it as little as possible. Start by adding flour, baking powder and salt together in a bowl. Mix ingredients. Chop butter into pea-size pieces. Rub into flour. Add milk to beaten eggs and add to dry ingredients. Barely mix the pastry.

Dump out on a lightly flour dusted board. Fold over pastry no more than 12 times. Flatten out pastry to about ¾-inches to 1-inch thick. Gently place on top of stew and bake for 25 minutes at 375 degrees, uncovered.

Remove from oven. Gently remove pastry from stew. Serve along with stew. Enjoy.

Jambalaya

In my opinion, jambalaya is one of the greatest Creole dishes ever created. Every Creole chef has their version and here is mine. The multitude of ingredients make this dish a pure flavour bomb.

Make sure you buy your shrimp uncooked with the shells still on, because you'll use the shells to flavour the stock. Andouille sausage (a heavily seasoned, smoked pork sausage) is a must, but if you can't find it, try using another good smoked sausage. Tasso ham is full of flavour, too. I even make my own and you can find my recipe on page 182. Again if you can't find it, use another good ham. Use other ingredients you like: the better the ingredients, the better the dish. You could try including pork, okra, crawfish and even rabbit. Have fun with it!

INGREDIENTS:

4 T olive oil

8 - 10 oz. andouille sausage, sliced

8 - 10 oz. tasso ham, cut in cubes

1 lb. chicken thighs, cut into ½-in. dice

1 t salt

½ t pepper

1 lb. uncooked shrimp with shells, peeled and deveined

2 cups chicken stock

1 t salt

3 bay leaves

1 T fish sauce

2 large onions, finely chopped

1 cup celery, finely chopped

2 T garlic, finely chopped

½ cup white wine

2 T Creole seasoning or blackening seasoning (page 260)

¼ t cayenne (optional)

1 T smoked or sweet paprika

1 cup long grain rice

1 cup canned fire-roasted chopped tomatoes

2 green bell peppers, chopped

2 green onions, finely chopped for garnish

In small saucepan, add shrimp shells, chicken stock, salt, bay leaves and fish sauce. Bring to a boil and turn off. Let shells poach in chicken broth. Set aside.

Heat oil in a large Dutch oven on medium heat. Add sausage and brown on both sides, remove to bowl and set aside. Season chicken with salt and pepper and add to Dutch oven. Brown for about 6 - 8 minutes. Add to bowl with sausages.

Now add onions and celery. Cook for another 8 - 10 minutes, stirring occasionally. Add garlic and cook for a couple of minutes. Add white wine and cook down until reduced by half. Add Creole seasoning (cayenne optional), rice, salt, strained chicken stock (discard bay leaves), ham and chicken mixture, tomatoes and peppers. Stir to bring everything together, cover and bring to boil; reduce heat to its lowest setting and simmer till rice is almost cooked and almost all the liquid is adsorbed, about 16 minutes. Add shrimp and cook for another 4 minutes till rice and shrimp are cooked. Add salt and pepper to your taste.

Quick Mediterranean Cod Stew

This is a very easy recipe. Use a shallow sauté pan. It will allow you to easily remove the loins without breaking them apart.

Serves: 4

INGREDIENTS:

4 cod loins (about 6 - 8 oz. each)
Salt and fresh ground black pepper
4 T olive oil
1 large onion, peeled and finely chopped
3 cloves garlic, finely chopped
½ cup white wine
28 oz. can whole tomatoes

½ cup kalamata olives, pitted
½ cup green olives, pitted
1 medium zucchini cut in half
    lengthwise, then in ¼-in. slices
1 t sea salt
½ t fresh ground black pepper

Heat a shallow, heavy-bottom sauté pan on medium-high heat. Add olive oil and sauté onion till soft, about 6 - 7 minutes. Add garlic and sauté for another minute.

Add remaining ingredients except the cod. Cover and let simmer for a couple of minutes.

Sprinkle a little salt and pepper on cod loins. Nestle the loins into sauté pan. Cover and simmer for about 10 - 12 minutes till cod is cooked.

Plate in a shallow bowl and serve with crusty bread.

Lobster Mushroom Ragout

I love both lobster and mushrooms, so I created this dish to celebrate them both, and it's become a favourite of mine. My one watch-out for this dish is to be careful with the type of mushrooms you use. Although button or cremini mushrooms are cheaper and will work, I highly recommend using oyster mushrooms, as they will truly give the dish a special taste and texture. They have a broad, thin, fan-shaped cap and tend to be clustered together. You should avoid the king oyster mushroom—this mushroom variety is not a good replacement. I like to use fresh lobster in season; however, if you are using frozen lobster, skip the first section of this recipe, and jump right into starting on the ragout.

Serves: 4

INGREDIENTS:

2 live lobsters (between 1 ½ - 2 lb. each)
1 gallon boiling water
½ cup sea salt
¼ cup olive oil, divided
1 lb. fresh oyster mushrooms, separated
1 large onion, finely chopped
4 cloves garlic, finely chopped
1 fresh red bell pepper, chopped
    into ½-in. chunks

¼ fresh Habanero, finely chopped, or
    more to your taste (I am in for 2 whole
    Habaneros, deseeded and finely chopped)
2 oz. brandy
1 T fish sauce
1 cup white wine
3 bay leaves
1 stick of butter
1 cup cherry tomatoes, cut in half
Reserved lobster meat and accumulated juices
Salt and fresh black pepper to taste

BOIL LOBSTER

To boil lobster, bring water to a boil in a large pot, and add sea salt. Add lobsters and bring back to the boil for 3 - 4 minutes. Remove lobster to cool. Discard water. Remove lobster from shells, reserving all liquid that drains from shells. You will add this to the finished stock later.

Start by removing the big claws and tail. Lay the tail on its side and use the heel of your hand to push down and crack the tail. Remove the meat. Split tail down back to form two even halves, forming the letter *C*. Remove intestine that runs down the tail.

Using a heavy cleaver, crack claws. Remove meat from shells, then remove the cartilage from the claws. Note: Lobster is still in a raw state at this point. This should yield about 1 pound of delicious lobster meat. Set aside till ready to use.

Now you can get started on the ragout.

Heat a heavy bottom-pot on medium heat then add a good drizzle of olive oil. Sauté mushrooms for about 10 - 12 minutes to remove excess water and brown the mushrooms. Remove from pan and set aside.

Add more olive oil and sauté onions for 6 - 8 minutes. Add garlic for an additional 2 minutes, stirring often. Add bell pepper and Habanero, and cook for 2 more minutes. Add previously sautéed mushrooms.

When heated through, add brandy and flambé. Stir in the fish sauce, wine and bay leaves. Add butter, tomatoes, lobster and accumulated juice in bowl. Simmer on low for 10 minutes to bring all the flavours together. Add salt and pepper to taste.

Serve in shallow bowls with some warm baguettes to sop up all the goodness.

Cajun Shrimp and Rice

As you will have now guessed, I really like Cajun flavours. I remember the first or second time I made this dish was with my dad. He watched me put two teaspoons of Tabasco sauce into the pot and then refused to eat it as it was deemed too spicy for him. I laugh about this now, as I often add Habaneros to my dishes to increase the level of heat. This is one of the only areas where I don't take after my dad.

This dish combines many of the ingredients I love and is all made in one pot, (except for the rice) so it's a quick clean-up for those doing the dishes. If you can find it, this dish works really well with pecan rice, which I used to buy at St. Lawrence Market on Front Street in downtown Toronto from Rube "the rice man's" stall, located down in the basement.

Serves 8 - 10

INGREDIENTS:

2 lb. raw shrimp, peeled and deveined (shells reserved)	3 T olive oil
3 bay leaves	1 lb. andouille or other smoked sausage, sliced
2 cups long grain rice, uncooked	1 lb. button mushrooms, sliced
5 cups chicken stock	4 onions, finely chopped
1 t salt	2 green bell peppers, diced
1 T Tabasco sauce	1 red bell pepper, diced
2 T Cajun seasoning (see page 260)	4 large cloves garlic, finely chopped
1 t paprika	½ cup green onions, finely chopped
	5 T fresh parsley, chopped

Bring chicken stock to a boil. Reduce heat to simmer and add reserved shrimp shells and bay leaves. Simmer for 4 - 5 minutes. Remove shells and bay leaves with a slotted spoon and discard. Stir in the salt, Tabasco sauce, Cajun seasoning, paprika and rice.

Cover and cook on low heat for 20 minutes till rice is done, or if using a different rice, cook according to package directions and set aside.

Next, while rice is cooking, heat a large Dutch oven on medium heat.

Add olive oil. Sauté sausage till browned on both sides. Add mushrooms and cook 4 - 5 minutes, stirring occasionally. Add onions and peppers and cook for another 4 - 5 minutes, stirring occasionally. Add garlic and cook for another minute or so.

Now add your shrimp and cook for a further 3 - 4 minutes till shrimp are cooked. Add cooked rice and remaining ingredients. Stir to incorporate everything together.

Pass the Tabasco sauce after plating for those who like more heat. Serve and enjoy.

Note: If you don't enjoy shrimp, feel free to substitute with diced chicken thighs instead.

Chicken and Cauliflower Casserole

I like to use real Parmigiano-Reggiano to make this dish, but you can use any cheese you like. If you're going with Parmesan, don't use the pre-grated stuff in a container. Buy the real deal and grate it yourself. You may never use any other cheese again.

Preheat oven: 375 degrees

INGREDIENTS:

6 cups cauliflower, separated into small florets
1 T salt
4 strips of thick cut bacon, cut into small pieces

1 lb. chicken (thighs or breast), cut in ½-in. pieces

Bring approximately 4 cups of salted water to a boil. Add the cauliflower and cook for 3 minutes. Remove to a bowl of cold water to stop the cooking process. Strain in a colander and set aside while you cook the bacon, chicken and make the béchamel sauce.

Heat a medium size Dutch oven on medium heat. Cook bacon till crispy. Remove with slotted spoon. Add chicken to the bacon fat and brown. Remove with slotted spoon.

Now make your béchamel sauce.

BÉCHAMEL INGREDIENTS:

1 stick butter
1 cup shallots or onions, finely chopped
3 cloves garlic, finely chopped
4 T all-purpose flour
1 t dry mustard
Pinch of cayenne
2 T chicken bouillon

1 t fish sauce (optional)
2 cups whole milk
2 ½ cups Parmigiano-Reggiano cheese, grated, or your favourite cheese (reserve ½ cup for the topping)
Salt and fresh ground pepper

BREADCRUMB TOPPING INGREDIENTS:

¾ cup fresh breadcrumbs
½ cup reserved grated Parmigiano-Reggiano cheese

¼ t fresh ground black pepper
Olive oil to drizzle on top

Reheat the same pot used to cook the bacon and chicken to melt the butter on medium heat. Add shallots and garlic and sauté till just soft. You are not looking to cook them fully or even brown them, just get them soft. Now add flour, mustard, cayenne, chicken bouillon and fish sauce. Stir to incorporate all the flour into the butter and shallots.

Slowly whisk in the milk, a little at a time, continuing to whisk. When sauce starts to bubble, it's time to stir in the cheese. Then, add salt and pepper to taste. Add chicken, bacon and cauliflower. Stir into the cheese sauce. Once fully combined, pour into a casserole dish.

Mix breadcrumbs, cheese and pepper together.

Top casserole with breadcrumb mixture. Drizzle olive oil on top. Bake in a preheated oven for about 30 minutes until the topping is browned and cheese is bubbling.

Let stand for 5 minutes before serving.

My Comfort Foods

Mac and Cheese

The key to making a great mac and cheese is choosing cheese you like. I love old cheddar, so most of my early mac and cheese dishes were made with old cheddar. I once had a full wheel of young Gouda. So, guess what? I made a Gouda mac and cheese and I think it was one of the best I ever tasted. You can even add a couple of ounces of a good blue cheese like Stilton to add a little funkiness. I like adding ham, but if you like, why not add some chopped lobster just before baking for an even more decadent dish? Your first step is to make a béchamel sauce. It's just a basic white sauce using butter, flour, milk and seasonings.

Preheat oven: 350 degrees

INGREDIENTS:

2 sticks butter

1 cup shallots, finely chopped

¾ cup all-purpose flour

2 T dry mustard

⅛ t cayenne powder

2 T chicken bouillon

1 T Worcestershire sauce

1 L whole milk

3 cups cheese of your choice, grated
   (reserve ½ cup for the topping)

1 t fine sea salt

½ t fresh ground pepper

2 cups of ham, cut into ½-in. chunks

Boil 1 pound of your favourite pasta according to package directions. I like using scoobi doo, otherwise known as cavatappi. Drain and reserve.

While pasta is boiling, start your cheese sauce, otherwise known as a béchamel sauce with cheese.

Melt butter on medium-high heat in a heavy-bottom pot. Add shallots and sauté till just soft. You are not looking to fully cook them or even brown them, just get them soft. Now add flour, mustard, cayenne, chicken bouillon and Worcestershire sauce. Stir to incorporate all the flour into the butter and shallots.

Now slowly whisk in the milk, a little at a time, continuing to whisk till you have added all the milk. When sauce starts to bubble, it's time to stir in 2 ½ cups of the cheese. Then add your salt and pepper. Add drained pasta and stir well.

If using ham or lobster, add and fold into dish now. Pour pasta into baking dish. Top with breadcrumb topping.

BREADCRUMB TOPPING:

1 cup fresh breadcrumbs

½ cup grated cheese (reserved)

½ t fresh ground black pepper

¼ cup olive oil

Mix reserved cheese and pepper into breadcrumbs. Top macaroni with the breadcrumb mixture. Drizzle with olive oil.

Bake in a 350 degree preheated oven for about 30 - 35 minutes till topping is browned and cheese is bubbling. Let cool for a few minutes. Serve and enjoy.

Broccoli and Cauliflower Casserole

You can use any cheese you like to make this dish. But my request is for you to make this dish just once with real Parmigiano-Reggiano cheese. Don't use the pre-grated stuff. Buy the real deal and grate it yourself. You may never use any other cheese again.

Preheat oven: 375 degrees

INGREDIENTS:

3 cups cauliflower, separated into small florets
3 cups broccoli, separated into small florets
1 T salt

Bring a pot of water to boil, about 4 cups, and add the salt. Now blanch the cauliflower and broccoli for just a few minutes. This ensures the vegetables will still be firm after baking and not turned to mush. Add the cauliflower to the salted water and cook for 3 minutes.

Remove cauliflower to a bowl of cold water to stop the cooking process. Add broccoli and cook for only 2 minutes. Again, remove to a bowl of cold water to stop the cooking process. Strain in a colander to remove all the water. Let sit while you make the béchamel sauce.

BÉCHAMEL INGREDIENTS:

1 stick butter
1 cup shallots, finely chopped
1 clove garlic, finely chopped
4 T all-purpose flour
1 t dry mustard
Pinch of cayenne

2 T chicken bouillon
1 t fish sauce (optional)
2 cups whole milk
2 ½ cups grated Parmigiano-Reggiano
    cheese (reserve ½ cup for the topping)
Salt and fresh ground pepper

Melt butter on medium-high heat in a heavy-bottom pot. Add shallots and garlic and sauté till just soft. You are not looking to fully cook them or even brown them, just get them soft. Now add flour, mustard, cayenne, chicken bouillon and fish sauce. Stir to incorporate all the flour into the butter and shallots.

Slowly whisk in the milk, a little at a time, continuing to whisk. When sauce starts to bubble it's time to stir in the cheese. Now it's time to add salt and pepper to taste. Add broccoli and cauliflower, and stir to cover with the cheese sauce. Pour into casserole dish.

Top casserole with breadcrumb mixture. Drizzle olive oil on top. Bake in a 375 degree preheated oven for about 30 minutes till topping is browned and cheese is bubbling.

BREADCRUMB TOPPING INGREDIENTS:

¾ cup fresh breadcrumbs

½ cup reserved grated Parmigiano-
   Reggiano cheese

¼ t fresh ground black pepper

Olive oil to drizzle on top

Mix breadcrumbs, cheese and pepper together.

Let stand for 5 minutes before you serve.

The No-Recipe Pot Roast

If you love a good pot roast, this is the recipe for you. It's really basic, and will please any crowd, anywhere. I have cooked this in some of the most sophisticated kitchens and rustic spaces known to man. It actually feels funny writing this recipe out, as it is really easy and should become something you love and don't need to think about. You can use a big chunk of beef or, if you have it available, a moose or caribou roast works wonderfully, too. The tougher the cut, the better.

To be honest, this brings back great memories for me of dinners with friends and family while hunting and fishing, and cozy nights with my wife in the middle of winter with the fireplace roaring. One of the more memorable times I cooked this meal was a few years ago on a snowmobile trip in March to Indian Bay, Newfoundland. It was the coldest winter I remember. After lunch, I told the guys I would get supper ready. In a rush, I popped the roast in my trusty cast-iron pot and added a bunch of chopped onions. I only had a package of beef OXO cubes, so in they went and I covered the roast with water. No browning—nothing. I placed it on the back of an old wood stove to simmer all afternoon. After a day of snowmobiling, we came back to the cabin starved. Everyone jumped in to peel the vegetables. The difficulty was waiting, especially with the aroma of this pot roast taking over the cabin. I pulled the roast into six pieces, piled on the vegetables and gravy, and served it with some homemade bread. Probably one of the most comforting meals ever.

Preheat oven: 275 degrees F

INGREDIENTS:

Any size roast (about 10 - 12 oz. per person, precooked weight, as the roast will shrink as it cooks)

4 - 5 large onions, peeled and chopped (you really can't use too many onions as they disintegrate into the gravy. Remember: onions mean flavour)

Root vegetables: a combination of carrots, potatoes, turnips (rutabaga), parsnips, all peeled and chopped into chunks

3 - 4 T flour

2 T tomato paste - add more if you are cooking a bigger roast

7 bay leaves

A good pinch of cayenne pepper

1 T salt (more if using low sodium stock or water)

Fresh ground black pepper to your taste

6 - 8 cups of braising liquid, enough to cover the roast (This can be a combination of what you have on hand or a single ingredient. I like to use dark beer, red wine or beef stock and sometimes all three. If you don't have any of those, water will do.)

Using a heavy-bottom pot large enough to hold your roast, all the onions and the vegetables, heat on medium-high heat. Add a little oil and brown the meat on all sides. Add the onions, cook for a few minutes, and stir in the flour and the remaining ingredients, except the vegetables.

Cover with the braising liquid, place your lid on the pot and bake for 4 - 5 hours on low heat at about 275 degrees. If you are available, occasionally check to ensure you have lots of stock; if not, add more.

Once the roast is almost tender, add the vegetables. Let simmer until they are tender, about 90 minutes. Tear roast into chunks and serve alongside the vegetables and gravy.

Serve with crusty bread rolls.

Bone-in Pork Chops with Mouth-Watering Gravy

There is nothing more satisfying than a meal that tastes great. I particularly love this dish because it's so simple and I love sucking the meat off the bones. Anytime I cooked this meal for my wife, Gayle, she always gave me her bones: a big bonus for me. You have to serve this dish with mashed potatoes and crusty rolls to sop up the delicious gravy.

Serves: 4

INGREDIENTS:

8 thin bone-in pork chops or 4 thick-cut ones
½ cup flour
2 t salt
1 t fresh ground black pepper
⅛ t cayenne powder
1 large ziplock bag

¼ cup olive oil
2 large onions, peeled and finely chopped
1 large clove of garlic, finely chopped
3 cups of pork or chicken stock
1 T fish sauce

Add flour and seasonings to Ziploc shaker bag. Shake to mix ingredients, then add pork chops to flour mixture in bag. Shake to cover all the pork chops with the flour mixture.

Heat a cast-iron pan or heavy-bottom pot on medium-high heat. Add olive oil and sear pork chops 3 - 4 minutes per side till browned. Don't overcrowd your pan. Remove from pan and set aside.

In the same pan, sauté onions 8 - 10 minutes till lightly browned. You may need to add more oil. Add garlic and sauté for another minute or so. Add remaining flour in shaker bag and stir into onions. Gradually add pork or chicken stock and fish sauce and stir to incorporate the stock into the flour.

Bring to a boil, return pork chops to the pan, and reduce to a simmer. Cover and simmer for about an hour till pork chops are very tender. Serve with mashed potatoes, peas and warmed crusty rolls.

Deep-Fried Fresh Cod or (Better Still) Halibut

I welcome the spring each year anticipating two things: lobster season and the opening of the cod fishery. I have spent many summer days jigging all over Newfoundland, which I enjoy with friends and family. But there is nothing like going with my sister Yvonne, who literally screams with joy when she catches a fish. It's even more fun when she hooks the bottom and I set the drag on her reel so she keeps reeling and reeling, thinking she has a monster on her hook. I sometimes get quite annoyed with her, but in truth, seeing such happiness makes her one of my favourite people to go cod fishing with.

Fresh cod or halibut deep-fried is a wonderful treat, especially when you catch it yourself. Here I have two versions. One has a very light batter; the second has a buttermilk and flour-only coating. I prefer the latter as the buttermilk soaks up the flour and you can enjoy the fish without the traditional heavy coating. Either way, brine the fish first before getting it ready for the fryer.

Serves: 4 - 6
Preheat fryer: 350 degrees

INGREDIENTS:

2 - 3 lb. fresh cod or halibut, cut into pieces

BRINE:

4 cups water (1 litre of water)
60 g fine sea salt (4 T)
20 g brown sugar (4 t)

In a large bowl, add cold water. Stir in sea salt and sugar. Stir until dissolved. Place fresh cod or halibut pieces in brine and let sit for about 20 minutes. While fish is brining, prepare fryer, and decide which version you want to cook. When brined, remove fish pieces to a paper-lined tray to drain.

LIGHT BATTER VERSION:

¾ cup flour
¾ cup corn starch
1 ½ t baking powder

½ t salt
1 (355 ml) can light beer

Whisk all ingredients together and let sit for 30 minutes. Batter should be relatively thin.

Preheat deep fryer to 350 degrees.

In a large ziplock bag, place about ½ cup of flour along with a little salt and fresh ground black pepper. Place a few pieces of fish in your bag and shake to cover with flour. Remove them from the flour and dip in your batter. Turn to cover both sides in the batter.

Let excess batter run off, then pop in your deep fryer for about 7 - 8 minutes depending on thickness. Deep-fry the thicker pieces first, then add the thinner ones a minute or two later to the fryer. Don't overcrowd the fryer. Serve with French fries. Enjoy!

FLOUR-ONLY VERSION:
1 cup buttermilk
1 cup of your favourite hot sauce (I prefer a piri piri sauce)

Mix buttermilk and hot sauce in a medium-size bowl.

Preheat deep fryer to 350 degrees. After brining, place dry fish pieces in buttermilk mixture. Remove the thicker pieces from the buttermilk mixture and place in a bag with about a cup of flour along with a little salt and fresh ground black pepper.

Shake to cover with the flour and deep-fry for about 7 - 8 minutes depending on the thickness. Add the thinner pieces to the fryer a minute or two later. Don't overcrowd the fryer.

Serve with French fries and enjoy!

Deep-Fried Chicken

One of life's guilty pleasures, I absolutely love to eat deep-fried chicken, but with heart disease in my family, I rarely used to indulge in it. When I was diagnosed with ALS, I was encouraged to eat high-fat foods and I took full advantage of this by eating many feeds of deep-fried chicken.

Serves: 4

INGREDIENTS:
1 (3 lb.) whole chicken cut into 8 pieces or 3 lb. of your favourite bone-in chicken pieces

BUTTERMILK BRINE:
3 cups buttermilk

¼ cup salt

1 T fresh ground black pepper

1 T sugar

7 bay leaves

SEASONED FLOUR MIX:
8 cups all-purpose flour

1 cup cornstarch

¾ cup fine sea salt

3 T fresh ground black pepper

2 T garlic powder

2 T onion powder

2 T paprika

2 T dry mustard

2 T dried basil

2 T dried thyme

2 T ground cumin

1 T ground ginger

1 T dried oregano

1 T cayenne powder

Mix all ingredients together and store in plastic container with a tight-fitting lid.

Mix together the ingredients for your buttermilk brine in a large bowl or ziplock bag. Add your chicken pieces and cover in the buttermilk brine. Let sit for a few hours or overnight.

When ready to deep fry your chicken, preheat fryer to 350 degrees.

Prepare a shaker bag by adding a little more than a cup of your seasoned flour mixture. Remove four pieces of your chicken from the buttermilk brine, shake off excess and place in the shaker bag with your seasoned flour mixture.

Massage the bag, pushing the seasoned flour into the chicken to ensure all the nooks and crannies get covered in the flour mixture.

Remove chicken from the bag one piece at a time, shaking off any excess flour, and lay on a plate. Then deep-fry the 4 pieces for about 15 minutes till internal temperature is 160 degrees F.

Check the internal temperature of the chicken at the 12-minute mark. Remove from fryer and place on a sheet pan with a rack layer on top and place in a warm oven. Keep in mind that the thicker breast and thighs pieces will take longer to cook than the drumsticks and wings.

I also use boneless chicken thighs skin on if I debone them myself. Cook for about 7 – 8 minutes.

Now cook remaining chicken pieces. Serve with French fries. Enjoy!

Easy BBQ Chicken and Vegetables

This is one of the easiest dishes I have ever created and made. I even made it for my in-laws on a small butane burner during a seven-day power outage in Toronto during the Christmas season of 2013.

Serves: 4 - 6
Preheat oven: 425 degrees

INGREDIENTS:

1 whole chicken, cut into 8 pieces, or about 3 lb. of your favourite bone-in chicken parts
1 (500 ml) bottle of your favourite BBQ sauce
3 large onions, finely chopped
4 large carrots, peeled and cut into chunks
6 celery stalks, cut diagonally into 1-in. chunks
2 T chicken concentrate
1 t fish sauce
2 t salt
1 t fresh ground pepper

For a healthier version of this dish, remove skin from chicken pieces and discard.

Now for the simplicity of this recipe.

Add chicken pieces, BBQ sauce, vegetables, chicken concentrate, fish sauce, salt and pepper to a casserole dish or heavy-bottom pot. Stir all ingredients.

Cover and bake in 425 degree preheated oven for 1 - 1 ½ hours. Remove cover after 30 minutes and stir. Serve with your favourite rice when chicken is fully cooked through.

Or if you wish, like I did during the power outage, simmer atop the stove on medium-low heat for about an hour again till chicken is fully cooked through.

Meatloaf

Meatloaf is an easy dish to pull together. The key is keeping it moist. I use beef stock, then add eggs and breadcrumbs to help keep it together. For a healthier option, you could add a cup of cooked quinoa to your meatloaf mixture and mix together as usual. If you wish, you can use a mixture of ground beef and pork. For Halloween, you can easily form your meatloaf into a mummy like I did. Have fun with it and create your own version.

Serves: 6 - 8
Preheat oven: 350 degrees

INGREDIENTS:

2 lb. medium ground beef	1 T dry mustard powder
2 T olive oil	1 ½ t fine sea salt
2 onions, peeled and finely chopped	1 t fresh ground black pepper
2 cloves garlic, finely chopped	⅛ t cayenne powder
½ cup beef stock	2 large eggs, beaten
2 T Worcestershire sauce	1 cup breadcrumbs
1 t fish sauce	1 cup ketchup (½ cup reserved to
1 t dried thyme	brush on top of meatloaf)

Heat a fry pan to medium-high heat. Add olive oil and sauté onion for 5 - 6 minutes till soft. Add garlic and sauté for another minute. Remove from heat and set aside to cool.

Add remaining ingredients including the onions and garlic to a large bowl, reserving half your ketchup for the top. Get your hands in there and mush everything together.

Using a rectangular casserole dish, free-form your meatloaf into a loaf. Push in the sides to help give the meatloaf height. Brush reserved ketchup all over meatloaf.

Bake in a preheated oven for 1 hour to an hour and 10 minutes. Check for doneness after an hour using a meat thermometer. Remove from oven at 150 - 155 degrees F. Let rest for 5 - 10 minutes before cutting. The meatloaf will gain about 10 degrees as it sits.

Serve with mashed potatoes and your favourite steamed vegetables.

Note: For my Halloween meatloaf mummy, I used onion pieces for the teeth, a cherry tomato for one eye and a rolled-up slice of prosciutto to mimic a worm crawling out of the other eye. I wrapped the head in regular sliced bacon. Brush the whole thing with your reserved ketchup: tastes great, and looks scary.

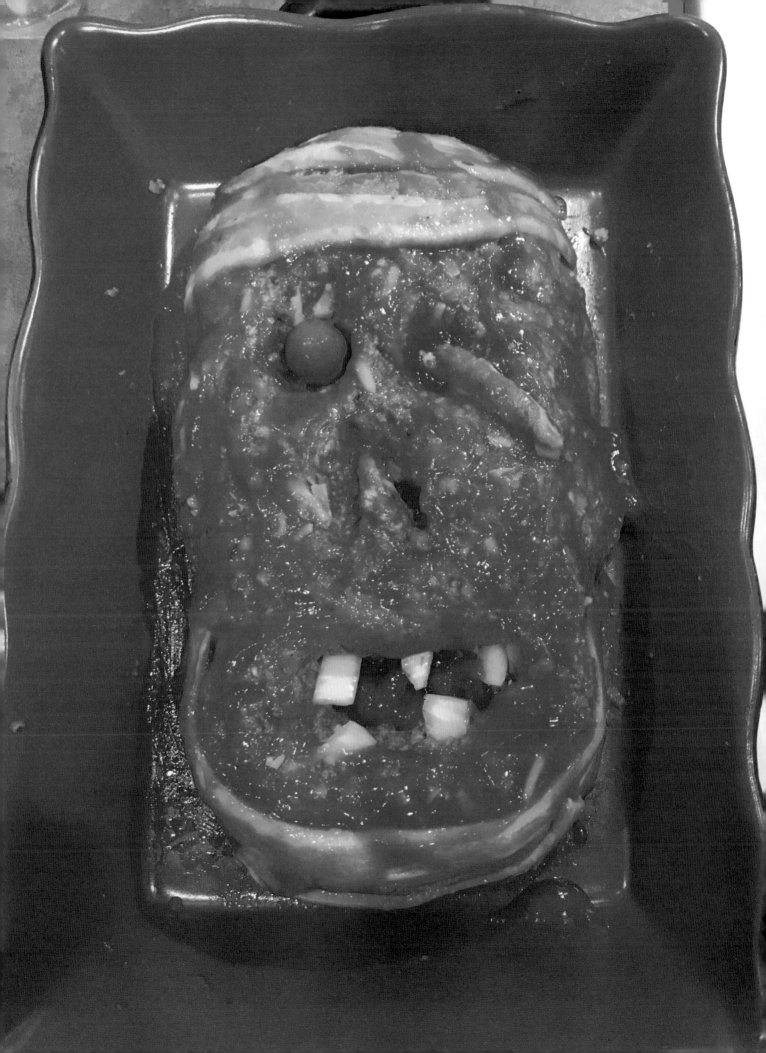

Baked Beans

The smell of baked beans cooking in my house normally means that there is a large family gathering about to happen or we have a good group of guests staying the night. So, needless to say, I have fond memories that go along with this recipe. Whether it is at your next family gathering, brunch or weekend at the cabin, I hope that you enjoy these beans as much as we have over the years.

INGREDIENTS:

1 lb. dry white beans	¼ cup black rum
6 - 8 cup water	2 t salt
2 medium onions, finely chopped	½ t fresh ground black pepper
½ cup ketchup	1 t Worcestershire sauce
½ cup molasses	1 t dry mustard
¼ cup brown sugar	½ lb. chopped meaty bacon

Rinse and sort beans. Occasionally, they may have a small stone or two. You don't want to chew on one of them. Wash in several changes of cold water.

Cover with cold water and let sit overnight. Otherwise, in a large pot, cover beans with cold water and bring to a boil on high heat. Turn off heat and let sit 30 minutes to allow beans to absorb some of the water. Put pot back to simmer on low heat for another 30 minutes. Meanwhile, prepare all other ingredients.

Preheat oven to 450 degrees.

Put onions, bacon, and all other ingredients into a bean crockpot. If you don't have a crockpot, any ovenproof pot will do. Add beans and enough liquid from beans to cover. Stir well.

Reserve the remaining liquid. Bake for 30 minutes.

Reduce temperature to 250 degrees. Bake for an additional 6 - 8 hours. After 6 hours, check beans and add reserved liquid as necessary to cover. Remove cover for the last hour of cooking to allow beans to thicken.

Turkey or Chicken Stuffing

Gayle's mother, Sybil, is of Scottish ancestry and she makes her stuffing from soda crackers and sage, but for me, a turkey or chicken is not the same without my stuffing. So when we cook a turkey together, she makes her stuffing and I make mine. We both take an end and stuff the turkey. She usually gets the cavity and I get the neck. I am happy with that because I get to have my stuffing and she hers. Thanks, Mom! We tried to take a picture of the stuffing but it didn't look like much, so you have a picture of a beautiful stuffed roasted chicken instead. It was yummy.

INGREDIENTS:

1 (340 g) bag fresh breadcrumbs
6 - 8 T dried savoury
½ t fresh ground black pepper
Pinch of cayenne powder

1 stick of butter (½ cup)
2 medium onions, finely chopped
½ cup chicken stock

Place breadcrumbs in a bowl, and add savoury, pepper and cayenne. Mix well. In a medium saucepan on medium-high heat, melt butter and sauté onions till soft, about 6 - 7 minutes. Add chicken stock. Pour over breadcrumbs. Mix well to incorporate all the dry breadcrumbs into the wet mixture.

At this point you want moist breadcrumbs, not wet ones. Stuffing is ready when all the breadcrumbs are slightly moistened.

This should be enough stuffing for a medium-size turkey in the 12 - 15 pound range or enough for two chickens. If you're cooking only one chicken, use half the stuffing and freeze the rest in the breadcrumb bag for another chicken later.

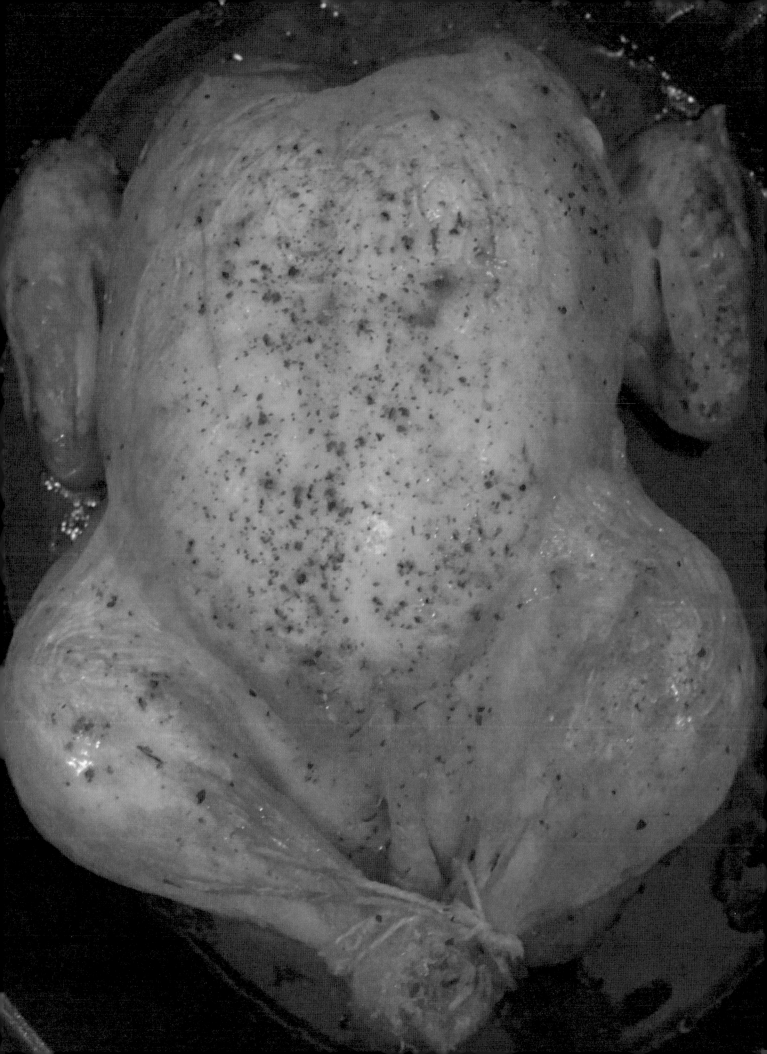

Pork Burgers

My wife is one of the only people I know who doesn't like beef hamburgers. I have tried several times to get her to try different versions, but each time was a dismal failure. That is until I made pork burgers and added HP Fruity Sauce on top. This simple burger has become a summer tradition and is one of the first things we BBQ for lunch when the warm weather arrives.

Makes: four 4-oz. burgers

INGREDIENTS:

1 lb. ground pork
3 T cold water
1 t fish sauce (optional)
Dash of cayenne pepper

1 t salt
Fresh ground black pepper to taste
4 soft dinner rolls
HP Fruity Sauce (optional)

Put the ground pork in a bowl. Mix the water and fish sauce together. Pour over pork. Sprinkle salt, cayenne and black pepper over pork. Mix well. Form into 4 flat patties.

Press your thumb in the middle of each patty. This will prevent the patties from forming into a ball as they cook. They should stay nice and flat like a burger patty should.

Grill on a preheated BBQ, 3 - 4 minutes per side. Right before your patties are cooked, cut dinner rolls in half and grill for a minute or so.

Note: I like to serve my pork burgers with HP Fruity Sauce. If you can't find it, use whatever condiments you wish. Sweet fruit sauces work well with pork.

Low and Slow

12-Hour Roasted Lamb Shoulder

I have a wood-fired pizza oven in my man cave, which reaches 1000 degrees F and can cook our pizzas in about 90 seconds. (They're delicious.) The oven holds its heat so much so that the next morning it is still about 150 degrees. One Sunday night, we had a pizza party and I decided to experiment by roasting a lamb shoulder after the pizzas were eaten while the oven was still hot. I popped the shoulder in the pizza oven before we went to bed and left it overnight. The next morning, I totally forgot about it, so it was there for about 20 hours by the time I removed it. Let me tell you: it was wonderful. I have since cooked it overnight and removed it after 10 to 12 hours. It's so delicious and tender, it literally falls off the bone. I know most people don't have a wood-fired pizza oven, so just pop in your regular oven overnight to get the same effect.

Preheat oven: 250 degrees F

INGREDIENTS:
1 whole bone-in lamb shoulder (6 - 8 lb.)

FOR THE BRINE:
3 - 4 quarts cold water, or just enough water to cover the shoulder
8 cloves garlic, peeled and crushed
2 dozen juniper berries, crushed
13 bay leaves

7 stalks of rosemary, crushed to release the flavour
Zest of 2 lemons and 2 limes
1½ cups sea salt
¾ cup brown sugar

Pour water in a container big enough to hold the lamb. Add all the brine ingredients. Let sit for an hour, stirring frequently to dissolve the salt and sugar. Place shoulder in brine refridgerated overnight but preferably 24 hours or longer, stirring occasionally. When brined, remove from brine and pat dry. Discard brine.

Place lamb shoulder on a rack in a roasting pan. Pour 2 cups boiling water in roasting pan. Cover lamb with parchment paper, which will prevent the salt in the lamb from eating through the foil. Then use foil to form a tight seal around the roaster. As an alternative, you could use a roaster with a tight-fitting lid.

Bake for 12 hours at 250 degrees F. Lamb should be falling off the bone. Remove the bones and place shoulder on a platter.

Drain the stock from the pan. Remove any fat from the surface. Bring to a simmer. Thicken it with a little cornstarch slurry. Continue to simmer for a few more minutes. Pour into a gravy boat. Serve family style, with copious amounts of oven-roasted root vegetables.

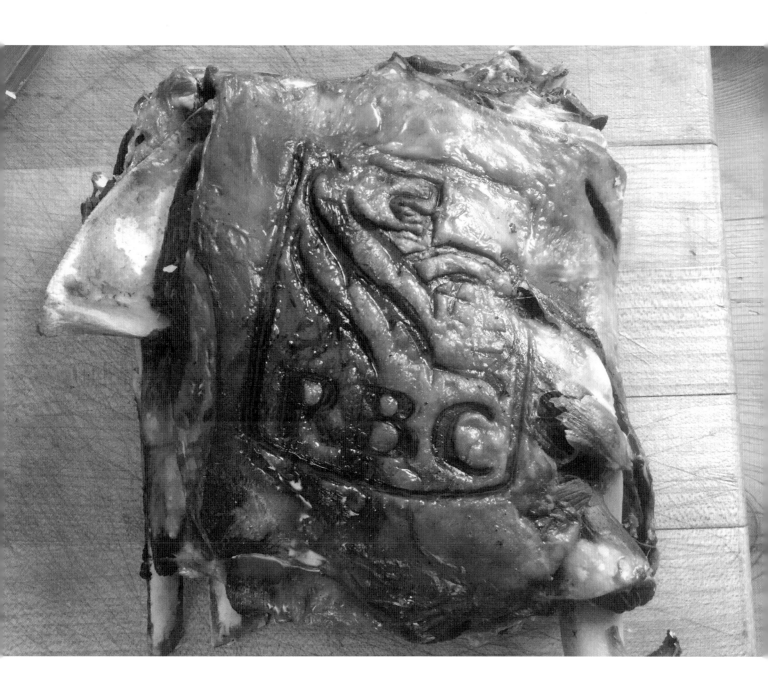

Slow-Braised Beef Cheeks

I think that for most people, beef cheeks are not a typical piece of meat they would bring home from the grocery store. Due to where it comes from on the cow, it is a very tough cut of meat, but with a decent amount of fat that ensures it has rich flavour. This tasty cut becomes very tender when slow-cooked. If you can't find beef cheeks, try a boneless beef shank—another very tough cut but very flavourful. I hope this recipe either reconfirms your love of this cut of meat or introduces you to a new option when considering your next beef meal.

Preheat oven: 300 degrees
Serves: 4 - 6

INGREDIENTS:

2 - 3 lb. of beef cheeks	2 large garlic cloves, finely chopped
½ cup flour	2 T tomato paste
1 T paprika	1 t fish sauce
2 t salt	1 T good soy sauce
2 t fresh ground pepper	2 cups red wine
¼ t cayenne	2 cups beef stock
1 large ziplock bag	3 bay leaves
¼ cup olive oil	2 large carrots, peeled and
2 large onions, finely chopped	chopped into chunks

You will start by cleaning the beef cheeks, removing most of the fat and the cartilage without removing too much of the meat. Cut your cheeks in half depending on the size. If they are small, leave them whole. Dry the beef cheeks.

Now add the flour and seasoning to your shaker bag. Shake to mix ingredients, then add beef cheeks to flour mixture in bag. Shake to cover all the beef cheeks with the flour mixture.

Next, heat a heavy-bottom pot on medium-high heat. Add olive oil and sear the cheeks. Do not overcrowd the pot. It is best to sear them in batches to ensure they get nicely browned.

Once all your cheeks are browned nicely, remove from pot and add chopped onions. Sauté for about 5 minutes while stirring occasionally. Add garlic and sauté for another minute. Add remaining flour in your shaker bag. Stir into onions.

You may need to add a little more olive oil. Add tomato paste and cook for another minute. Now add the remaining ingredients, except the carrots, and bring to a light simmer. Add cheeks and cook until tender, about 2 - 2 ½ hours. (An alternative is to bake in a 300 degree oven till tender.) Add carrots in the last hour of cooking time.

Remove cheeks from pot and keep warm. Discard bay leaves and reduce stock until it is nice and thick.

Serve on a bed of mashed potatoes along with the carrots and the delicious sauce. Enjoy.

Slow-Cooked Hanger Steak

Hanger steaks were commonly known as the butcher's steak. There is only one per steer and most butchers didn't bother to sell it, but cooked it for themselves instead. It's a great cut of beef if you can find it.

Serves: 4

INGREDIENTS:

2 hanger steaks (about 1 lb. each)

½ cup good olive oil

2 large onions chopped

2 large finely chopped garlic cloves

2 T tomato paste

1 t Red Boat fish sauce

1 T good soy sauce

1 cup red wine

2 cups good beef stock

3 bay leaves

Salt and fresh ground black pepper to taste

A couple of dashes of cayenne

Clean hanger steaks by removing most of the fat and the cartilage down the middle without removing too much of the meat. Cut into pieces. In a heavy-bottom pot, heat on medium-high heat. Add olive oil, dry meat and sear. Do not overcrowd the pan. Sear and brown nicely in batches.

Once all steak is browned, remove from pan and add chopped onions. Cook for about 5 minutes while stirring occasionally. Add garlic, tomato paste, salt and pepper, and cook for another minute. Add remaining ingredients and bring to a light simmer. Add steaks, bring back to a light simmer and cook till tender.

Remove steaks from pot, and reduce stock till nice and thick. Alternatively, add a slurry of water and corn starch to thicken sauce. Remove and discard bay leaves.

Enjoy as a main course served on a bed of polenta or with your favourite veggies.

Oven-Roasted Beef Short Ribs

Oftentimes, the beef short rib gets a bad rap as a tough, fatty cut of meat. Yet, restaurants serve them up for a small fortune. Why not cook them yourself? The trick here is time. You need to cook beef short ribs for at least three hours to ensure you get them tender and render the fat off. This is a great recipe for a Saturday or Sunday afternoon when you are mucking around the house and have the time to simmer the ribs in the oven. It is also a great meal for hosting a dinner party, as once the ribs are finished cooking in the oven the actual BBQ time is short, leaving you the opportunity to enjoy time with your guests. You can even bake the ribs a few days in advance. Refrigerate till the day you want to BBQ them, then remove them from the refrigerator about an hour before you plan to grill them, so they come to room temperature. If you wish, skip the BBQ altogether. Just reheat the ribs in the sauce and serve with your favourite sides.

Preheat oven: 300 degrees
Serves: 4

INGREDIENTS:

5 - 6 lb. beef short ribs (about 6 in. long)	3 bay leaves
¼ cup olive oil	1 bunch fresh thyme
1 large onion, finely chopped	1 T brown sugar
2 carrots, peeled and finely chopped	¼ t cayenne powder
4 large cloves garlic, finely chopped	1 t fresh ground black pepper
3 T tomato paste	1 T paprika (preferably smoked)
1 bottle red wine	2 t salt
1 cup beef stock	

Heat a heavy-bottom pot on medium-high heat. Add olive oil and sear the ribs in batches so you don't overcrowd the pot. When browned, remove to a plate. Add onions and carrots and sauté for about 6 - 8 minutes. Now add your garlic and sauté for another minute or so. Stir in your tomato paste.

Add the remaining ingredients including your ribs and bring to a boil. Cover your pot and transfer to oven. Bake for 3 hours at 300 degrees F until tender. When your ribs are tender, remove pot from oven. Remove the ribs from your pot. Spoon and discard all the accumulated fat from the sauce. Remove and discard your bay leaves and thyme stalks.

Using a handheld immersion blender, process your sauce till it reaches a smooth consistency. Serve sauce along with your ribs and mashed potatoes or your favourite sides.

If you decide to serve your ribs BBQ style, reduce your sauce until it reaches the consistency of a BBQ sauce. Store your sauce in a container in the refrigerator. Store the ribs in the refrigerator, as well, till the day of your BBQ.

When ready to BBQ, preheat your BBQ to 350 - 400 degrees.

Remove the ribs from the refrigerator for about an hour to come to room temperature before grilling.

Grill for 12 - 15 minutes brushing with the sauce till warmed through. Serve with your favourite sides or consider the Cajun corn recipe on page 262.

Oaxacan Lamb Barbacoa

This recipe makes for extremely tender lamb that is great for tacos, quesadillas or enchiladas or served as a main dish with oven-roasted potatoes. Use whole-dried ancho chili peppers, stems and seeds removed, roasted and freshly ground, or a good ancho chili powder. Regular chili powder is not a good replacement for the ancho chili powder but if it's all you have, go ahead and use it.

Preheat oven: 325 degrees

INGREDIENTS:

1 (4 - 6 lb.) bone-in lamb shoulder or
   3 - 4 lb. cubed lamb shoulder
2 T olive oil
2 medium onions, chopped
4 large cloves garlic finely chopped
6 T ancho chili powder
2 T smoked sweet paprika
1 T oregano
1 t cumin
1 T sea salt

1 T dark brown sugar
1 oz. unsweetened chocolate or high cacao
   content chocolate, chopped (i.e. 80 - 90%)
1 cup orange juice
1 T fish sauce (optional)
2 cans dark beer like Guinness
7 bay leaves
1 large stick of cinnamon or
   1 t ground cinnamon

Heat a Dutch oven large enough to hold the lamb shoulder on medium-high heat. Add the olive oil and brown the lamb shoulder. Turn the shoulder bone-side down in Dutch oven. Set aside.

Add remaining ingredients except the beer, bay leaves and cinnamon stick to a food processor. Process till smooth. You may need to add a little beer to get a smooth consistency.

Pour the purée over the shoulder. Add the bay leaves and cinnamon stick to the pot. Pour the remainder of the beer around the pot. Do not disturb the purée on the lamb shoulder.

Bake covered in preheated 325-degree F oven for 4 - 5 hours until meltingly tender. Check after 3 hours and baste frequently. Remove lamb from oven. Thicken sauce if necessary.

Remove bones and discard. Shred lamb in the Dutch oven if using in your favourite taco or enchilada recipe. If not, serve chunks of lamb as a main course with oven roasted potatoes.

BBQ Baby Back Ribs

I love any type of BBQ ribs. However, this recipe is not for your standard slow-cooked ribs, smothered in a sweet BBQ sauce. One day at the supermarket, I was looking for a pork loin to throw on the BBQ. I always seem to pick up every piece of meat in the case before I eventually make my purchase. This day I noticed that the bone-in pork rib roast was cheaper than the loin by itself. So I bought it, knowing I saved money and I got a few pork ribs for free. I can't recall what I did with the loin that evening for supper but I sure remember what I did with the ribs. Not having the usual two to three hours to slow-smoke and smother them in BBQ sauce, I did something a little different. I just added salt, pepper and garlic powder. Then I dry-roasted them on the top back rack of the BBQ for about an hour and a half or so on indirect heat. I sprayed them occasionally with a little apple juice mixed with water. They weren't your usual fall-off-the-bone tender, but they were porky and delicious.

Preheat BBQ: 400 degrees with only one side of your BBQ lit

INGREDIENTS:

1 rack of baby back ribs, cut in half
    (membrane removed from the back)
Salt

Pepper
Garlic powder (optional)
Apple juice mixed with a little water

Place ribs meat-side down on a cutting board. Remove the membrane from the back of the ribs by gently inserting a butter knife between a bone and the membrane. Pick a bone in the middle. Be gentle and wiggle the knife. Get your finger between the bone and the membrane. Work your finger down the bone and eventually get a second finger in there. Pull membrane off and discard.

Cut ribs into 2 pieces. Shake desired amount of salt and pepper, more than you think is necessary, and garlic powder if using.

Place your prepared ribs on the top rack of BBQ without any direct heat under it (i.e. heat on one side, ribs on the other side). Cook with the lid closed to maintain a temperature of about 400 degrees.

Over the next 60 - 90 minutes, depending on how much meat is on the ribs, turn them every 10 - 15 minutes. Each time you turn your ribs, spray the ribs using a spray bottle filled with a mixture of apple juice and water to keep them moist.

You know they are done when the ribs "give" slightly when you insert a fork between the bones.

These are not your usual fall-off-the-bone ribs. These have a nice gentle bite to them. But because they are dry-roasted with only minimal ingredients, they are a wonderful way to experiment with baby back ribs in a pinch. Serve alongside your favourite sides.

BBQ Baby Back Ribs - Take Two

Looking to speed up the process one evening, I decided to try cooking the ribs in foil with apple juice. It worked very well. Try it.

Serves: 2
Preheat BBQ: 300 degrees

INGREDIENTS:

1 rack baby back ribs or St. Louis style side ribs
5 - 6 T dry rub seasoning mixture
   (see recipe on page xx)

¾ cup apple juice
½ cup of your favourite BBQ sauce

You should remove the membrane on the back of the ribs to help the dry rub penetrate the ribs. Place ribs meat-side down on a cutting board. Remove the membrane from the back of the ribs by gently inserting a butter knife between a bone and the membrane. Pick a bone in the middle. Be gentle and wiggle the knife. Get your finger between bone and the membrane. Work your finger down the bone and eventually get a second one in there. Pull membrane off. Discard. Cut ribs into 2 pieces.

Shake the dry rub all over both sides of ribs and rub in. Get about 2 feet of foil wrap and fold in two. Place ribs one on top of the other meat-side up on the foil wrap. Fold foil together to make a tight package. Leaving one end open and pour in the juice. Fold foil to seal package.

Place on top rack above heat and bake for about 2 hours undisturbed while maintaining your 300 degrees. (If using St. Louis style side ribs, give them an additional half hour.) After 2 hours, remove ribs from foil reserving any juice. Pour juice into cup with BBQ sauce.

Reduce heat to 200 degrees F.

Brush ribs 2 - 3 times in the next 10 - 15 minutes, then remove and serve alongside your favourite sides.

Pasta Dishes

Lobster with Angel Hair Pasta

This was a dish I created to impress my wife, Gayle, on one of her first visits to Newfoundland. I jokingly say she is one of nine people actually born and raised in Toronto, and I knew her Achilles heel was pasta. So, I decided to create this very special pasta with lobster for her. I didn't know that she didn't like lobster. Like, who doesn't like lobster? Well, my sister Yvonne and Gayle are (I think) the only two people on earth who don't. To make matters worse, I chose a type of pasta I'd never worked with before: bucatini, a long macaroni type of pasta that looks like straws on steroids when it's cooked. Five or six of these babies on the plate is a meal in itself. It really didn't help that I cut the lobster in large chunks to match the monster-pasta-fire hoses. Well, that evening's dinner didn't go well. Suffice to say, I have since redeemed myself by cooking Gayle her favourite spaghetti and meat sauce.

Since making this disaster, I now use a more appropriate base of angel hair pasta. And no, Gayle still doesn't like it, but it has been a hit at many dinners for lobster-lovers across Canada.

Serves: 4
Preparation and cooking time: 25 minutes

INGREDIENTS:

2 live lobsters (between 1 ½ - 2 lb. each)
4 quarts boiling water
½ cup sea salt
½ stick butter
1 large onion, finely chopped
3 cloves garlic, finely chopped
1 oz. cognac
1 cup white wine
¼ cup heavy cream

1 t fish sauce (optional)
⅛ t cayenne pepper
½ t fresh ground black pepper
Reserved lobster and juices
2 cups cherry or grape tomatoes, cut in half
½ lb. angel hair pasta
1 cup Parmigiano-Reggiano
    cheese, freshly grated

Let's start by boiling the lobsters. Bring 1 gallon of water to boil in a large pot, and add ½ cup of sea salt. Add lobsters and bring back to the boil for 4 - 5 minutes. Remove lobsters to cool.

Remove lobster meat from the shells, reserving all liquid that drains from shells. You'll add this liquid to your dish later. Remove cartilage from claws. Split tail down the back to form even halves that form the letter C. Remove intestine that runs down the tail. Chop lobster in small pieces, roughly ½-inch in size. This should yield about 1 pound of delicious lobster. Add chopped lobster to bowl with reserved liquid and set aside.

Note: Lobster is still in a raw state at this point.

Let's pull the dish together.

In a large pot of boiling salted water, cook ½ lb. of angel hair pasta till al dente or according to package directions. Drain and set aside.

Heat butter in a heavy-bottom pot on medium-high heat. Add onions and cook for 5 - 6 minutes. Add garlic and cook for another minute while stirring. Deglaze pan with the cognac. Add remaining ingredients except the cheese.

Reduce heat to simmer and cook for about 5 minutes to bring all the flavours together. Add the cooked angel hair pasta and cook to your preference. Stir in Parmigiano-Reggiano cheese. Serve and enjoy.

Chicken and Pasta in White Wine Cream Sauce

This is a quick and easy pasta dish for a weekday dinner that will fill your belly and delight your taste buds.

Serves: 6 - 8

INGREDIENTS:

4 large chicken breasts, skinless, boneless, sliced thinly

4 T olive oil

4 T butter

½ lb. cremini or button mushrooms, finely sliced

3 onions, finely chopped

4 cloves garlic, finely chopped

2 oz. brandy

½ cup white wine

1 t fish sauce (optional)

½ cup chicken broth

¾ cup heavy cream

Salt and pepper to taste

Dash of cayenne pepper

Bring a large pot of salted water to a boil and cook 3 cups dry penne pasta or your favourite pasta. Cook pasta al dente. Set aside while preparing the chicken sauce.

In a heavy-bottom pot, sauté the chicken breast pieces in olive oil and butter until brown. Remove from pan.

Sauté mushrooms 5 - 6 minutes. Add onions and sauté till soft, about 8 more minutes. Add garlic and sauté for an additional minute. Add brandy, white wine, fish sauce, chicken broth and cream. Add back chicken and mushrooms, then add salt, fresh ground black pepper and cayenne.

Simmer covered for 5 minutes.

Add pasta to sauce and cook till pasta is cooked to your preference. Serve.

Spicy Squid Ink Pasta with Shrimp and Chorizo

This is a very interesting pasta dish: not anything out of the normal but delicious all the same. If you can't find yellow tomatoes, go ahead and use the red ones. If you don't like heat, skip the red pepper flakes.

Serves: 4

INGREDIENTS:

½ lb. squid ink pasta

1 lb. raw shrimp, peeled and deveined (reserve peels)

8 oz. dry Spanish chorizo

½ cup olive oil

3 large shallots, peeled and finely chopped

8 cloves garlic, peeled and thinly sliced

3 bay leaves

½ cup white wine

1 lb. yellow grape or yellow cherry tomatoes

1 t red pepper flakes

1 t paprika

1 t fish sauce

2 t sea salt

1 t fresh ground black pepper

Bring a pot of salted water to a boil and cook the squid ink pasta till al dente or according to package directions. Set aside 1 cup of the pasta water. Drain pasta and set aside.

Remove casing from chorizo if you can, then coarsely chop chorizo. Place in a food processor and pulverize till finely chopped. Set aside.

In small saucepan, add shrimp shells along with the reserved pasta liquid, white wine and bay leaves. Bring to a boil and turn off heat to let shells poach in the white wine stock. Set aside.

Coarsely chop half the shrimp, leaving the other half whole. Heat half the olive oil in a heavy-bottom sauté pan over medium-high heat for a couple of minutes. Add the whole shrimp and sauté about 1 minute per side. Remove to plate. Add the chopped shrimp and saute for a minute or so all the while stirring. Remove the chopped shrimp to the plate with the whole shrimp.

Add remaining olive oil and sauté chorizo and shallots for 3 - 4 minutes till shallots are soft. Add sliced garlic and sauté for another minute or two.

Using a slotted spoon, remove and discard shrimp shells and bay leaves from saucepan. Add white wine stock and yellow tomatoes to sauté pan and sauté till tomatoes start to break down. Add red pepper flakes, paprika, fish sauce, salt and pepper. Add your al dente pasta and cook to your liking. Add back shrimp and stir to warm through. Serve.

Pasta with Chicken, Garlic and Habaneros

A special meal doesn't need to be complex. I was recently reminded of this simple pasta dish when my son Christopher, who lives in Australia, emailed to ask me for the recipe. He described it as "that pasta dish you used to make for us with a white wine sauce and Habaneros, it was nothing fancy." I raised my sons, Colin and Christopher, to eat everything, so I was pleasantly surprised when this was a dish Christopher remembered and wanted to make in his thirties. Simple can be memorable.

Serves: 4

INGREDIENTS:

1 ½ lb. boneless skinless chicken thighs, cut in ½-in. pieces
1 ½ t salt
½ t fresh ground pepper
3 T olive oil
1 onion, finely chopped
6 large cloves garlic, finely chopped

1 Habanero, finely chopped (ribs and seeds removed)
1 cup white wine
½ cup chicken stock
1 t fish sauce (optional)
1 cup Parmigiano-Reggiano, fresh grated
½ lb. angel hair pasta (or your favourite pasta)

Bring a pot of salted water to a boil and cook pasta to al dente or according to package directions. Strain the pasta and reserve it for later.

Meanwhile, add oil to a hot sauté pan. Season chicken with salt and fresh ground black pepper and brown in a hot pan about 7 - 8 minutes. Add onions, and sauté for an additional 5 minutes. Add garlic and chopped Habaneros, and sauté for a few more minutes. Add wine, chicken stock and fish sauce.

Increase heat to a boil, then reduce to a simmer for a couple of minutes. Now add reserved pasta and stir for a few minutes to finish cooking the pasta to your preferred doneness and liquid is reduced to a sauce. Stir in Parmigiano-Reggiano. Serve immediately.

Note: Feel free to omit the Habanero if you don't like heat or add a couple if you love the heat, like I do.

Baked Penne Pasta with Chicken and Cheese

This is an easy baked pasta dish that you can make pretty quickly after a long work day or prepare it early on a Saturday morning and hold it until dinner time to bake it. I have also provided a version you can make when you are serving many people at one time. I find this dish is kid-friendly, so it's really good as a family meal.

Preheat oven: 375 degrees
Serves: 4

INGREDIENTS:

3T olive oil
1 lb. of boneless chicken breasts or
    thighs, cut into small pieces
1 t salt
½ t fresh ground black pepper
Pinch of cayenne
1 medium onion, finely chopped
3 cloves garlic, finely chopped

½ cup white wine
½ cup chicken stock
½ t fish sauce (optional)
2 sweet peppers, coarsely chopped
½ lb. penne pasta (or your favourite)
2 cups old cheddar cheese, cut in ½-in. cubes
1 cup old cheddar cheese, grated

Bring a pot of salted water to a boil and cook pasta to al dente according to package directions. Strain the pasta and reserve it for later.

Heat oil in deep fry pan. Add chicken and sauté for 5 - 6 minutes. Add salt, pepper, onions and garlic. Sauté for a few more minutes. Add wine, stock, fish sauce and bring to a simmer. Add sweet peppers, stir and simmer for a minute or two. Remove from heat and set aside.

Add drained pasta to your pan with the chicken. Stir for a few minutes. Add cheese cubes and stir again.

Add pasta and chicken to your baking dish, cover with grated cheese and bake for 25 minutes at 375 degrees or until browned nicely.

Note: I suggest penne pasta but any small-shaped pasta will work here. I love Habaneros, so I add a finely chopped Habanero before baking. As well, small broccoli florets can be added to the pasta before baking, if desired.

Pork Loin in Fire-Roasted Tomato Sauce with Pasta

I am not really sure why I started making this dish. I guess it was because my wife loves pasta and I am a carnivore. This dish allows me to have my meat with a little pasta and my wife the opportunity to have her pasta with less meat.

Preheat oven: 400 degrees
Serves: 4

INGREDIENTS:

1 lb. pork loin, thinly sliced
¼ cup olive oil
3 medium onions, finely chopped
4 sticks celery, finely chopped
2 carrots, peeled and chopped in ¼-in. dice
3 cloves garlic, finely chopped
1 (28 oz.) can fire-roasted diced tomatoes

1 (14 oz.) bottle fire-roasted tomato sauce
½ cup red wine
1 t fish sauce
⅛ t cayenne pepper
Salt and fresh ground black pepper to taste
8 oz. Parmigiano-Reggiano
   cheese, freshly grated

Prepare half a pound of your favourite pasta according to package directions. Drain and set aside.

In a large heavy-bottom pot, heat the olive oil and fry the pork in batches until browned. Remove the pork from the pot.

Sauté the onions, celery, and carrots for approximately 10 minutes. Add your garlic and sauté for another minute or so. Return the pork to the pot and add the fire-roasted diced tomatoes and the fire-roasted tomato sauce. Add the red wine, fish sauce, cayenne pepper, salt and pepper. Simmer on low heat for about an hour and a half till sauce has thickened to your liking.

Add your desired amount of pasta to the bottom of a single-serving casserole dish or pasta dish. Add the meat sauce on top. Top with ¼ of the cheese. Bake for 20 minutes till the cheese has melted. Enjoy!

Shrimp with Angel Hair Pasta in a Tomato Gorgonzola Sauce

This is a wonderful, rich and creamy pasta that can be done with shrimp or chicken. I have written this recipe using shrimp because that's what I prefer, but if you're allergic to shellfish or just not a fan, you can easily replace the shrimp with the chicken cut of your choice.

INGREDIENTS:

1 lb. uncooked shrimp, peeled and deveined
4 T butter
4 shallots, finely chopped
3 cloves garlic, finely chopped
¼ cup brandy
½ cup white wine
½ cup chicken stock
3 bay leaves

2 cups good tomato sauce
8 oz. Gorgonzola cheese, crumbled
1 t fish sauce
⅛ t cayenne pepper
½ t red pepper flakes (optional)
Salt and pepper to taste
½ lb. uncooked angel hair pasta

In small saucepan, add shrimp shells, chicken stock and bay leaves. Bring to a boil and turn off. Let shells poach in chicken broth. Set aside.

Cook ½ lb. of angel hair pasta according to package instructions. Drain and set aside.

Meanwhile, melt butter over medium heat in sauté pan. Add shallots and garlic to sauté for a few minutes. Add brandy and flambé. Add wine and cook until reduced by half. Add remaining ingredients including chicken stock (discard bay leaves), except shrimp. Bring to a simmer and cook for 8 - 10 minutes to bring all the flavours together.

Now, add shrimp to sauté pan and cook for 3 - 4 minutes (depending on the size) to cook the shrimp. Next, add pasta to sauté pan with the shrimp. Stir in and let sit together for a few minutes.

Serve hot.

Slow-Cooked Beef Shank
with Rigatoni

This recipe works well with any cut of beef, but the tougher the cut, the better. Honestly, you can't get a tougher cut of beef than the shank, bone in and full of connective tissues. You will be amazed at the deep rich flavour that you just can't get from a more expensive cut of beef. You can serve chunks of the shank with mashed potatoes and vegetables or shred and serve it with your favourite pasta, as I did the last time we made it. This recipe will take time but it's well worth it. That reminds me, the last time we cooked it, Gayle and I left Toronto and drove east to Big Rideau Lake just southwest of Ottawa. We arrived at our friends Wally and Valerie's place at about 4:30, beef shank in tow, to have for supper that night. Needless to say, we ate late and we ate well that night.

Serves: 8

INGREDIENTS:

5 - 6 lb. bone-in beef shank	2 cups red wine
½ cup good olive oil	2 cups beef stock
2 large onions, peeled and chopped	5 bay leaves
2 carrots, peeled and finely chopped	2 t salt
5 large garlic cloves, peeled and finely chopped	1 t fresh ground black pepper
1 small can of tomato paste (about 5.5 oz.)	¼ t cayenne powder
1 (28 oz.) can tomatoes	1 lb. of rigatoni or your favourite pasta
1 T Red Boat fish sauce	Chunk of Parmigiano-Reggiano cheese

In a heavy-bottom pot (preferably oval to fit the shank easily), heat on medium-high heat. Add olive oil and sear. Sear shank and brown on all sides. Remove from pot and set aside.

Now add your chopped onions and carrots. Cook for about 5 minutes while stirring occasionally. Add garlic, tomato paste, salt and pepper, and cook for another minute. Add the remaining ingredients and bring to a boil. Add beef shank, bring back to a light simmer and cook till tender, about 4 - 5 hours.

Check the shank after 3 hours, and every half hour or so thereafter. When the shank is starting to show signs of tenderness, remove cover and reduce stock till nice and thick.

While the shank is cooking, prepare and cook your preferred pasta to al dente and set aside till shank is done.

Remove and discard bay leaves. Remove the shank bone and shred the shank. When sauce has thickened to your liking, add previously-cooked pasta and heat in the meat sauce till done to your liking.

Plate your beef shank pasta and pass the cheese along with a grater for your guests to help themselves to enjoy atop their pasta. Otherwise, pass a bowl of freshly grated Parmigiano-Reggiano.

Seafood Dishes

Mussels with Queso Fresco

I love mussels and they are cheap, too. When you buy them, make sure they are fresh. If most are gaping open, take a pass as many of them may be dead. You can serve this dish as an appetizer or add a side salad (or frites for French Moules et Frites) as a main course for one person. Simply double the recipe for two people. The key with mussels is to make sure you wash them well and remove any shells that do not close when you tap them before cooking.

Serves: 1

INGREDIENTS:

1 lb. fresh mussels, washed
2 T butter
1 small onion, finely chopped
¼ cup of chorizo, finely chopped
2 cloves garlic, finely minced
1 Thai chili, finely minced

¼ cup white wine
2 bay leaves
1 t fish sauce
Juice of ½ lime
4 T crumbled Queso Fresco cheese
Fresh ground pepper to taste

Aggressively wash the mussels in several changes of cold water. Get both your hands in and aggressively move the mussels around, rubbing the shells together. Your water should look murky at this time. Rinse and repeat till water is clear.

Now it's time to pick over the mussels. Any that are open may be dead and should be discarded. To check if the mussel is dead or alive, give the shell a tap against a hard object. If it's alive, it will slowly start to close, so it's good to keep. If it's doesn't close, discard it.

The opposite is also true once the mussels are cooked. Any mussels that remain closed after cooking should be discarded as they are dead. Don't attempt to open them, just discard immediately. Only use the mussels that have opened wide.

Melt butter in heavy-bottom pot, add chorizo and onions and sauté for 2 minutes. Add garlic, chili, and sauté for another minute. Add wine, bay leaves, fish sauce, lime juice and mussels, and simmer, covered, for 7 - 8 minutes, till mussels have all opened, shaking pot occasionally.

Plate mussels, discarding bay leaves and any unopened mussels. Top with cheese and serve with crusty bread.

Fresh Poached Cod Loins and Potatoes

If you don't have fresh cod, skip this recipe immediately. You will be very disappointed with frozen cod. Full fillets of fresh cod will work fine but the thicker loins work best. If you're using full fillets, separate the loin and cut the remaining fillet in two pieces. In a perfect world, I would cook a half pound of salt beef, cut in smaller pieces, simmered in boiling water for about two hours, and then use this water to poach the fish and potatoes. Instead, to speed up the process for this recipe we are using only the sea salt. I hope you enjoy this dish as much as I do.

Serves: 2

INGREDIENTS:

6 - 8 cups water (just enough water to cover your fish)
1 ½ - 2 lb. fresh cod loins (haddock will work quite fine as well)
2 eggs, soft boiled
2 large potatoes, peeled and cut into slightly large chunks
1 medium onion, peeled, cut in half and thinly sliced

3 bay leaves
1 T butter
1 T sea salt
1 small clove garlic, slightly crushed with the side of your knife
Butter for topping cod and potatoes (lots of butter)
Fresh ground black pepper, if desired

Bring water to boil in a wide shallow pan. The shallow pan will allow you to remove the delicate poached cod in one piece without breaking it apart. Add sliced onion, bay leaves, butter, salt and garlic.

Cover and simmer for a few minutes to develop a flavourful poaching liquid. Increase heat to medium, add potatoes and cook for 8 - 10 minutes till about half done.

Add cod and eggs. Poach cod 5 - 7 minutes depending on thickness. If using full fillets, separate the loins and poach for a few minutes before adding the thinner pieces. Poach eggs for 5 - 6 minutes. Remove from the heat and peel.

Using an egg turner or large slotted spoon, remove cod, potatoes and onions to serving plates. Top the cod and potatoes with copious amounts of butter. Cut eggs in half and add to plate. Top with fresh ground black pepper if desired.

Roasted Halibut with Jerusalem Artichoke Purée and Butter-Poached Lobster

I love Jerusalem artichokes and created this dish for a charity dinner I cooked for a few years back. Jerusalem artichokes are a hard-to-find ingredient so you have to plan ahead to make this recipe. It also takes time with many specific steps, but if you are looking to impress a group of dinner guests, it is worth the planning and the time.

Serves: 8
Preheat oven: 425 degrees to roast your lobster shells; 550 degrees for the halibut

INGREDIENTS:

2 lb. Jerusalem artichokes
¼ cup butter
Salt and pepper to taste
4 live lobsters (1 - 1 ¼ lb. each)
1 gallon boiling water
½ cup sea salt
3 carrots, chopped
3 celery stalks, chopped
2 onions, chopped
2 cloves garlic, crushed
3 T tomato paste
6 bay leaves

1 t whole black peppercorns
½ cup sherry or port
1 cup white wine
2 lb. mixed wild mushrooms
4 T butter
2 T olive oil
Salt and pepper to taste
1 lb. salted butter
8 six-ounce portions of fresh halibut filet
2 T olive oil
Salt and pepper to taste

ROAST ARTICHOKES:

Preheat oven to 375 degrees. Scrub artichokes and cut away any black spots. Cut in half or into even-size pieces. Melt butter in a medium-high pan and brown all cut sides, about 6 - 8 minutes. Transfer to parchment-lined baking sheet and roast till fork tender, about 25 minutes. Remove from oven and set aside to cool. Transfer to food processor. Add salt and pepper to taste and a little butter. Purée till smooth. Set aside and keep warm.

BOIL LOBSTER:

To boil lobster, bring water to boil in a large pot, and add sea salt. Add lobsters and bring back to the boil for 3 - 4 minutes. Remove lobster to cool. Discard water. Remove lobster from shells reserving all liquid that drains from shells. You will add this to the finished stock later.

Start by removing the big claws and tail. Lay the tail on its side and use the heel of your hand to push down and crack the tail. Remove the meat. Split tail down back to form two even halves, forming the letter C. Remove intestine that runs down the tail.

Using a heavy cleaver, crack claws. Remove meat from shells, then remove the cartilage from the claws. This should yield about 1 pound of delicious lobster meat. Note: Lobster is still in a raw state at this point.

MAKE LOBSTER STOCK:

Now place all the shells including the bodies in a roasting pan. Add chopped vegetables and garlic. Stir in the tomato paste. Roast in preheated oven (or roast the shells on your BBQ to avoid the smells wafting through your house) for about an hour. Browning the shells and the vegetables will add colour and flavour to the end stock.

Place the roasted shells and vegetables in a stockpot. Add the bay leaves and peppercorns. Add sherry and white wine to roasting pan, scraping any brown bits from the pan. Pour into stockpot.

Add about 10 cups of boiling water to wash out the roasting pan. (Do not use the water you previously used to cook the lobsters; it's too salty.) Add to stockpot.

Remove cover and simmer for at least an hour, preferably two hours. Stir stock occasionally and use a potato masher to mash the shells and vegetables. Strain the stock through a sieve and reserve. Discard the shells and vegetables.

Strain stock into a small pot, adding reserved liquid from lobster shells (when you removed the lobster from the shell) and reduce to about 2 cups. Remember that we have not added any salt as of yet, so season to your taste. You will need to thicken the stock with a little cornstarch slurry. Set aside and keep warm till ready to plate.

SAUTÉ MUSHROOMS:

Melt butter in frying pan, add olive oil, mushrooms, salt and pepper and sauté till browned and no liquid remaining. Set aside and keep warm till ready to plate.

POACH LOBSTER:

Melt 1-pound block of butter in a saucepan barely big enough to fit the lobster. Poach lobster tails for about 3 minutes, then add claws and continue for another minute or so. Lobster should be completely submerged in butter. Cover and set aside till ready to plate.

BAKE HALIBUT:

Preheat oven to max temperature, preferably 550 degrees convection. Place halibut, evenly spaced apart, on baking sheet lined with parchment paper. Brush with olive oil, then season with salt and fresh ground pepper. Bake for about 9 minutes till cooked. Halibut should be firm but still give slightly to the touch. Remove from oven and begin plating.

PLATING:

Using a shallow, wide bowl, evenly distribute artichoke purée by adding about 4 tablespoons of artichoke purée in centre of bowl. Place halibut on top of the purée. Next place ½ lobster tail, cut-side down. Then place claw on top of tail followed by ¼ cup of the lobster stock. Add sautéed mushrooms atop lobster and around bowl and serve.

Halibut with Black and White Barley

If you can find it, buy a box of barley blend—a mix of hull-less white barley and parboiled black barley. It's bigger than pearl or pot barley and has a great bite. I use halibut as the fish here but you can easily swap it for other white fish like cod or haddock. If you do, use the thicker loin section. You want to allow extra time to prepare this dish, as the tomatoes take about four hours to dry.

Serves: 4

INGREDIENTS:

4 eight-ounce portions of halibut
6 plum or roma tomatoes
½ t fine sea salt
3 T butter
1 medium onion, peeled and finely chopped
1 large carrot, peeled and cut into ¼-in. dice
2 cloves garlic, finely chopped
1 cup uncooked black and white barley

4 cups chicken stock
Salt and fresh ground black pepper
8 oz. of slab bacon or 5 - 6 slices of thick
    cut bacon cut in ½-in. pieces
1 cup lobster stock - see page 52
2 t cornstarch
1 cup micro greens (optional)

PREPARE TOMATOES:

Preheat oven to 225 degrees F. Cut tomatoes in half lengthwise. Using a sharp knife, cut a *V* in the tomato where it was attached to the stem. Discard. Prepare a sheet pan with a rack and lay tomatoes cut side up. Sprinkle a little salt on each tomato. Put tomatoes in the oven, using the lowest rack.

Bake for about 3 - 4 hours till tomatoes are somewhat dried. They should be still soft and pliable, shrivelled around the edges but still somewhat plump at the same time. Set aside.

PREPARE BARLEY:

Melt butter in a saucepan on medium heat. Add onion and carrot and sauté for 5 - 6 minutes. Add garlic and cook for another minute. Add chicken stock, a little salt and fresh ground black pepper and bring to a boil. Add barley and reduce heat to a simmer.

Cook for 50 - 60 minutes till tender but firm. It will still be a little chewy. Check after 45 minutes. You may need to add more stock. When done, set aside and keep warm.

FRY THE BACON:

If using slab bacon, cut in ¼-inch slices. Then cut the slices into ¼-inch lardons or matchsticks. Add bacon to a cold frying pan. Cook bacon on medium heat for about 10 minutes till crispy. Remove bacon to a paper-lined bowl and keep warm.

PREPARE LOBSTER SAUCE:

Heat lobster stock. Mix a couple of teaspoons of cornstarch in ¼ cup of water. Add a few teaspoons at a time to the lobster stock to thicken the sauce. Set aside and keep warm.

BAKE HALIBUT:

Preheat oven to max temperature, 550 degrees convection. (I use convection to maximize heat and cook the halibut without drying it out.) Place halibut evenly spaced on baking sheet lined with parchment paper. Brush with olive oil, then season with salt and fresh ground black pepper.

Bake for about 9 minutes till just cooked. Halibut should be firm but still give slightly to the touch. Remove from oven and begin plating.

PLATING:

Using a shallow, wide bowl. Evenly distribute barley by adding about ½ cup in centre of bowl. Place halibut on top of barley. Place 2 pieces of dried tomato and sprinkle bacon on top and around dish. Next place a few microgreens on top. Finish by pouring about ¼ cup of lobster sauce around base of bowl.

Prosciutto-Wrapped and Stuffed Jumbo Shrimp

One Saturday afternoon in July, friends called to ask if I would like to come for supper at their summer home. "Sure," I said and, "what's for supper?" Kevin responded by saying, "Don't know yet." Since it was the end of the lobster season, I offered to bring lobster as we all loved it. So, off I went to my favourite fishmonger, Judy, to get some lobster. Well, it definitely was the end of the season, and to my horror, she was sold out of lobster. Now what to do? I settled on some of the biggest shrimp I had ever seen. I forget their size, but I think they were about six ounces each. And that was just the tail. They were monsters.

En route to Kevin and Dale's place, I was wondering how we could cook these very large shrimp. Here is what we did: I think it's one of the best dishes Dale and I ever created.

Serves: 6

INGREDIENTS:

½ medium Spanish onion, finely chopped
2 sticks salted butter
2 cups mushrooms, finely chopped
2 large cloves garlic, finely chopped
4 T fresh thyme leaves, finely chopped
½ cup fresh breadcrumbs

A good pinch of cayenne pepper
Salt and pepper to taste
1 cup good white wine
6 jumbo shrimp tails
¼ cup Dijon mustard
6 slices prosciutto

Start by sautéing onions in ¼ stick of butter for about 5 minutes until soft. Add mushrooms and the remaining ¾ stick of butter. Sauté, stirring often for about 10 more minutes to cook and reduce water from the mushrooms. Add garlic, thyme, breadcrumbs and cayenne. Stir to combine and cook 5 more minutes, adding more butter as required. Set aside to cool while preparing shrimp.

Peel shrimp, but save the shells. Add the shrimp shells to a pot just big enough to hold them. Add 1 cup white wine and bring to a boil. The goal here is to infuse the wine with the shell flavour.

Reduce the wine to about ½ a cup. Drain and reserve the wine for later.

Meanwhile, cut shrimp down the belly without cutting all the way through. This will allow you to stuff them easily. Devein if necessary. Spread Dijon mustard generously over cut side of shrimp. Lay out a piece of prosciutto and lay shrimp sort of crossway or diagonally on the prosciutto.

Stuff with cooled stuffing and wrap in prosciutto using toothpicks to hold if necessary. Continue until all shrimp are stuffed.

Heat a fry pan on medium-high heat. Add ½ stick of butter. When the butter is melted, add shrimp. When butter begins to brown, pour in reserved wine-flavoured shrimp stock. Cover and cook for about 5 minutes. Remove cover and brown the shrimp.

By now, most of the wine should have evaporated. Add a little more butter if necessary, cooking for an additional 2 minutes. Remove and serve. Total cooking time will depend on the size of the shrimp so don't overcook them. You'll know shrimps are done when they feel firm to the touch.

We made a pot of jambalaya to go with our shrimp that evening and we ate like kings. Our menu also included seared foie gras on toast points with Granny Smith apples, sautéed in Calvados. For dessert we made crepes with maple syrup, glazed apples and vanilla ice cream. And, yes, there was some wonderful wine, so I stayed over for the night.

Hope you enjoy!

Miso-Marinated Atlantic Cod

This is a classic Japanese seafood preparation made famous by Chef Nobu Matsuhisa. Although his restaurant uses only black cod, any white fish like Atlantic cod, haddock or halibut will work. You could even use salmon, too. Try to use a thicker cut like the loins. Do try to marinate your fish for at least a few days. You and your dinner companions will be impressed by the result.

Serves: 4
Preheat oven: 450 degrees

INGREDIENTS:

4 cod loins about 8 oz. each (or whatever fish you plan to use)
5 oz. sake or white wine
5 oz. mirin

½ t fish sauce
3 T white sugar
1 dash of cayenne powder
1 cup white miso paste

Put the sake or white wine, mirin, fish sauce, sugar and cayenne in a saucepan. Bring to a boil, then reduce heat to a simmer. Let simmer for about 7 minutes. Remove from heat and let cool. Add sake mixture to a bowl, add miso paste and whisk well until the mixture is very smooth.

Cut your fish into serving-size pieces if not already done. Put in a ziplock bag and pour in the miso marinade. Move fish around in the bag to ensure the marinade is covering all the fish and that your fish is laid flat. Refrigerate for at least 24 hours, but preferably longer, for 48 - 72 hours.

Preheat a cast-iron pan on stove top on medium-high heat for 3 - 4 minutes. Add a little oil to pan. Scrape the marinade off one side of the fish and place that side down in your hot pan.

Sear for 2 - 3 minutes till lightly browned. Flip the fish over onto a heavy rimmed parchment-lined baking sheet and roast for about 7 - 8 minutes, depending on thickness, until done and fish flakes.

Transfer to plates and serve with oven-roasted asparagus. They can be cooked on the same sheet pan as your cod. Otherwise you can lightly sauté some baby bok choy with fresh sliced garlic and serve with your cod.

Canning, Curing and Sausage Ideas

Pickled Beets

There really isn't anything like fresh produce that you can pickle and enjoy all winter long. Pickling beets is a long-held tradition that comes with your annual harvest in the fall. I used to pickle beets years ago and I recently started again when we planted a vegetable garden in our backyard.

INGREDIENTS:

8 lb. of beets

PICKLING INGREDIENTS:

2 ½ cups apple cider vinegar   3 T pickling salt or sea salt
3 ½ cups white sugar   3 T pickling spices
2 ½ cups water   1 (3-in.) stick of cinnamon

Bring all pickling ingredients together in a pot to a boil. Then reduce heat, cover and simmer for 30 minutes. Remove from heat and set aside.

Wash beets. Cut stems off leaving about 1 inch attached to the beets. This will prevent the beets from bleeding too much of their colour in the water. Place beets in a pot and cover with cold water.

Cover and bring to a boil, then reduce heat to medium. Depending on size of beets, cook 30 - 45 minutes till tender. A fork inserted in a beet should easily pierce the beet. Plunge beets in a pot of cold water and when cool enough to handle, slip off the skins.

Cut beets into desired size pieces, usually ½-inch - ¾-inch chunks. Put cut beets back in the pot. Strain pickling liquid into beets and bring to a boil.

Turn off the heat the moment your pot reaches a boil. Spoon the beets into prepared jars, then laden the hot pickling liquid to cover beets keeping ½-inch headspace. Top with lid and screw cap tight.

Allow to cool undisturbed. As they begin to cool, they will seal. You will hear them pop. They are now vacuum sealed. When you push down on the lid, it will be tight. Any that springs back have not sealed and should be consumed first. The others will keep for months.

Pickled Mustard Seeds

These pickled mustard seeds are simple to make and go great on sandwiches or served as part of a charcuterie board.

INGREDIENTS:

¾ cup yellow mustard seeds
¼ cup black mustard seeds

FOR THE BRINE:

1 cup brown sugar
2 t sea salt
½ cup white wine

1 ½ cups apple cider vinegar
½ cup cold water

Add all ingredients for the brine in a saucepan. Bring to a boil, then reduce heat to a medium low.

Add mustard seeds and simmer uncovered for about 30 - 35 minutes. The seeds will plump up and the liquid will reduce and thicken.

Pour mustard seeds and any liquid remaining into a covered jar. These pickled mustard seeds will store for many months refrigerated.

Boudin Blanc

Boudin blanc is a classic French sausage or pudding made with chicken or pork, eggs and cream. This is a very light and delicate sausage, nothing like the Boudin blanc made in Louisiana which is generally made with pork, liver, rice and heavily spiced. Boudin blanc is generally made around Christmastime and because of the spices used, it tends to taste and smell like Christmas, too.

Yields: about 30 six-inch sausages

INGREDIENTS:

1 lb. fatty pork belly, cut into small cubes
1 lb. pork shoulder, cut into cubes
2 lb. chicken thighs, chopped small
3 T butter
1 large onion, peeled and finely chopped
2 t white pepper (6 g)
⅛ t cayenne
⅛ t freshly grated nutmeg
⅛ t ground cloves

⅛ t ground cinnamon
3 T fine sea salt (40g)
1 oz. cognac
16 large eggs
3 cups whole milk
200 g panko breadcrumbs
2 cups whipping cream
16 - 20 feet of natural hog casing

Heat a fry pan to medium heat. Add butter and sauté onions for 6 - 7 minutes till soft. Set aside to cool.

Grind your meats using the fine die of your meat grinder. Then add your ground meat, cooked and cooled onions to the bowl of a stand mixer. Add your spices, salt and cognac and using the paddle attachment, and combine meat with your spices for about 30 seconds. Alternatively, you can chop your meats very fine in a food processor.

Slowly beat in eggs one at a time followed by the milk, then add the breadcrumbs. Now add the cream and stir till just combined.

Fry a little piece of your sausage to check for seasoning. Adjust if necessary.

Stuff the sausage into your casings. Twist at 6-inch intervals. Every second sausage, twist in the opposite direction.

Poach sausages in a pot of hot water (about 170 - 175 degrees F) for about 30 minutes. Do not let the water come close to a boil as the sausages will burst. After 30 minutes, check the internal temperature of a sausage. Remove from pot at 160 degrees F internal temperature.

To serve, sauté in butter on medium-low heat till lightly browned and warmed through.

Bottled Mussels

Bottling mussels is not an easy job, but these mussels are so much better than store-bought ones bottled in vinegar that it's worth the effort. So, when you're ready to tackle this recipe, try and enlist some help. If not, prepare yourself for a few long hours of a laborious task.

I tend to do things in a big way, so one summer day, I bought a 35 pound bag of mussels from my fishmonger, Judy. It was much more work than I had expected. The good thing was once the job was done, I had lots of bottles to enjoy and give away. You can start small if you wish. Four pounds of mussels in the shell will yield you about one pound of meat. This recipe is for a reasonable amount: 20 pounds of mussels in the shell, which should yield you about 5 pounds of meat to bottle. If you are brave enough, next time you can cook 35 pounds!

INGREDIENTS:

20 lb. of mussels in the shell (will yield about 5 lb. of mussel meat)
2 cups dry white wine
15 bay leaves
2 cups shallots, finely chopped

3 large cloves garlic, crushed
Dash of cayenne
3 T sea salt
1 t fresh black pepper

FOR BOTTLING:

2 - 3 cups mussel stock reserved
½ cup white vinegar

1 cup white wine

Aggressively wash the mussels in several changes of cold water. Start by adding about 3 - 4 lb. of mussels to a bowl or in your sink and half cover with cold water. Get both your hands in and aggressively move the mussels around rubbing the shells together. Your water should look murky at this time. Rinse and repeat till water is clear. Drain, reserve and wash the remaining mussels the same way.

Now it's time to pick over the mussels. Any that are open may be dead and should be discarded. To check if the mussel is dead or alive, give the shell a tap against a hard object. If it's alive, it will slowly start to close, so it's good to keep. If it's doesn't close, discard it.

The opposite is also true once the mussels are cooked. Any mussels that remain closed after cooking should be discarded as they are dead. Don't attempt to open them, just discard immediately. Only use the mussels that have opened wide.

Depending on how many mussels you're cooking, you may have to cook them in batches. If you have never cooked mussels, you will be surprised by how little water or wine you need to cook them. The reason is that the mussels are closed tightly and are holding a fair amount of water in the shell. All this water is released during the cooking process, creating a ton of wonderful tasting broth.

Let's get cooking. In large pot, add wine, bay leaves, onions, crushed garlic cloves, cayenne, salt and pepper. Bring to a boil. Let simmer for a few minutes. Add mussels to fill about half the pot. Reduce heat to medium high and cook for about 8 minutes. Remove cover and stir mussels. They should all be wide open and firm.

Remove mussels to a large bowl. Continue cooking remaining mussels. When all mussels are cooked, reserve the cooking liquid.

Now for the hard work: time to shuck the mussels. It's important for me to say again that any shells that are closed are dead and should be discarded. Many of the mussels fall out of the shell, saving you time. Those that are still attached require more effort. Generally the mussel is dislodged from one side of the shell and only attached by the big muscle (the adductor muscle) on the other shell.

Tear off the top empty shell. Using your thumb, push your thumbnail down under the big adductor mussel and the mussel should come off the shell easily. Now keep going—you only have a thousand more to go! Any onions in the shells can be saved along with the mussels and bottled along with them.

Once you get all the mussels removed from the shells, it's time to start bottling them. I like to use the 8 oz. (250 ml) jars for bottling mussels. Prepare a dozen bottles just in case. If you are only cooking 4 lb. of mussels, you will only need four 4 oz. (125 ml) jars, hardly worth the effort.

It's time to start filling your jars. I put a bay leaf in the bottom of each jar. Next, top up each jar with mussels, leaving about ½ inch of head space. Add 1 tablespoon of white vinegar and 2 tablespoons of white wine per jar. Bring 2 - 3 cups of the mussel stock back to a boil and add a little to each jar, again keeping the ½ inch of head space.

Put a lid on each jar and screw the band tight. Place a rack in the bottom of a pot. Cover the rack with about ½ inch of boiling water. Place jars on top of rack and steam for 90 minutes to 2 hours. Before steaming them, ensure the water level is about half way up the side of the jars. Keep your heat on medium to keep a good steam going.

The water inside the jars should be boiling before you take them off the heat. Keep an eye on the water level of your pot. Keep water about half way up the side of your jars. If you have to add water, add boiling water.

After removing them from the pot, tighten the jars again. As they begin to cool, they will seal. You will hear them pop. They are now vacuum-sealed. When you push down on the lid, it will be tight. Any that spring back have not sealed and should be consumed within a few days. The others will be good for a few months refrigerated.

Enjoy.

Bottled Smoked Oysters

Smoking oysters is a process well worth the reward at the end. These are nothing like the small cans you find in the supermarket. I use pre-shucked Fanny Bay oysters from BC. They are packed in one or two pound plastic containers. I brine them overnight, then poach them for a few minutes the next day to firm them up. Next, they hit the smoker for an hour or so for a light smoke and then I bottle to preserve them.

Here we will start with four 1-lb. containers. Be prepared for weight loss. I started with 80 oysters, weighing 64 ounces. After brining, I was down to 60 ounces. After poaching, I was down to 44 ounces and down to 34 after smoking. That's essentially half the weight I started with. If you love smoked oysters, you might want to double the quantity of oysters. I would double the brine but use the same amount of poaching liquid. Just poach in five to six batches.

Let's get started.

STEP 1. PREPARE BRINE.
INGREDIENTS:

4 lb. pre-shucked oysters, drained

FOR THE BRINE:

4 cups cold water
4 T fine sea salt

2 T white sugar

In a large bowl, add water, sea salt and sugar. Stir till salt and sugar has dissolved. Add drained oysters and brine overnight refrigerated. The next day, remove oysters from brining liquid. Reserve oysters and discard brine.

STEP 2. PREPARE TO POACH THE OYSTERS.
INGREDIENTS:
FOR POACHING LIQUID:

½ cup dry vermouth
1 cup white wine
1 ½ cup water

1 t salt
½ t white sugar
5 bay leaves

Add the six poaching ingredients to a shallow sauté pan. Bring to boil. Add half of the oysters. Bring poaching liquid back to a boil, then remove oysters with a slotted spoon and set aside. Bring to boil again and add remaining oysters. Bring poaching liquid back to a boil, then remove the oysters to bowl with previously poached oysters. Reserve poaching liquid.

STEP 3. SMOKE THE OYSTERS.
INGREDIENTS:

¼ cup olive oil

Poached oysters

Piece of cherry or maple wood

Pour the olive oil over the poached oysters and stir to cover.

Line a rimmed sheet pan with parchment paper. Place a cooling rack atop the parchment paper. Place the oysters on the rack, making sure they're not touching each other.

Prepare your smoker, or in my case, a propane BBQ. I wrap a chunk of cherry or maple wood in several layers of foil, then poke a bunch of large holes in the top. Remove cooking rack and place foil-wrapped wood directly on BBQ grate. Light only the burner under the wood. Keep all other burners off. You are not looking to cook the oysters any further, just smoke them. When your wood starts to smoke, place the tray with your oysters on the opposite side of your BBQ.

Smoke the oysters for an hour or so. Try to keep the heat in the 175 - 200 degree F range, no higher. If you have a smoker, you know how to regulate the temperature. After about 30 minutes, check the oysters. If they have taken on a nice smoke colour, turn them over for another 30 minutes or so.

Once smoked, remove them from the smoker/BBQ and set aside. Smoke remaining oysters. Set all the smoked oysters aside. Drain any accumulated juices from the parchment paper and add about a cup of the poaching liquid. Reserve.

STEP 4. BOTTLE THE OYSTERS.

You will need approximately twelve 125 ml jars or six 250 ml jars. Ensure jars and lids are clean. Allocate the oysters between the jars keeping about ½-inch headspace free. The small jars should hold 5 - 6 oysters, the large ones 11 - 12 oysters. Put 2 tablespoons of the reserved liquid in each small jar or 4 tablespoons in the larger jars. Put a lid on each jar and screw the band tight.

Place a rack in the bottom of a pot. Cover the rack with about ½ inch of boiling water. Place jars on top of rack and steam for 90 minutes.

Keep your heat on medium to keep a good steam going. The water inside the jars should be boiling before you take them off the heat. Keep an eye on the water level. Keep water about halfway up the side of your jars.

After removing them from the pot, tighten the jars again. As they begin to cool, they will seal. You will hear them pop. They are now vacuum-sealed. When you push down on the lid, it will be tight. Any that springs back have not sealed and should be consumed within a few days. The others will be good for a few months refrigerated.

Home-Cured Bacon

Curing your own bacon is not that difficult, and it's a good way to control the amount of salt, sugar and smoke you're eating. The two main ingredients you need are pork belly and sodium nitrite, generally referred to as pink curing salt or Prague powder. Do not use pink Himalayan salt, it's not the same thing. Prepare to be overwhelmed by the accolades. You may never eat store-bought bacon again. After you have cured your bacon, you have to cook it. This is normally done by smoking at a low heat and cooking it at the same time. You need to smoke with hardwood. My preferences are cherry, apple, oak and maple wood.

BASIC CURE:

450 g fine sea salt (almost 2 cups)
250 g brown sugar (about 1 ¼ cups)

60 g pink curing salt* (4T)

Mix all ingredients and store in airtight container. Use as needed and store remaining cure for another use. There is enough cure here for about 30 pounds of bacon using the salt box method below.

For this recipe, I am suggesting you start with a 4 - 5 pound piece of pork belly, skin removed. The weight really doesn't matter. Trim the belly to square up the edges. You will use the basic cure above to rub all over your pork belly. Then fit it into a ziplock bag in a single layer and store it in your refrigerator for about 6 - 7 days. Depending on how much pork belly you are curing, you may need to cut your pork belly in half and use two bags.

Your pork belly will be cured using what's called the salt box method. Using a flat-bottom glass dish or non-reactive dish, add about ½ cup of the basic cure to your dish. Rub each piece of pork belly on all sides to absorb as much cure as will stick to it, shaking off any excess. Push the pork belly into the cure. Continue adding as much dry cure to the dish as you need to ensure all sides of your pork belly get an even coating.

Put your pork belly in a ziplock bag and refrigerate for about 6 - 7 days. If your bacon is a thinner slab, 5 days should be fine. The key to when it is cured is when the pork is no longer soft and squishy. It should be firm to the touch, much firmer than when you started.

Every day you should turn your bacon over to help distribute the cure evenly. You will notice a little liquid accumulate in the bag. This is normal. The cure is taking a little water from the pork belly.

After about 7 days, your cure has now done its job. Remove from bag and rinse under cold water and pat dry. Place pork belly on a rack and let it dry for 4 - 6 hours refrigerated or overnight to form a pellicle, or thin skin. It should feel dry or tacky to the touch.

Now it's time to smoke your bacon.

Smoke on your smoker or you can use your BBQ. Smoke for about 2 - 3 hours depending on thickness. Preheat BBQ to about 200 degrees F.

If you don't have a smoking unit, no worries. Take a chunk of hardwood, wrap in foil, remove the grill and put directly on the burner of your BBQ. Poke a bunch of holes in the top of the foil to let the smoke escape. Turn burner to high. Turn most of your remaining burners off. Try to maintain around 200 degrees F in your smoker or BBQ.

When smoke appears, reduce the heat under your chunk of wood to about medium. Place your bacon on a rack away from the heated side of your BBQ and smoke using indirect heat. Let it smoke for between 2 and 3 hours, checking occasionally and turning your bacon from time to time.

Check internal temperature at the 2 hour mark. You are looking for an internal temperature of 150 degrees F.

When you have reached the 150 degrees F internal temperature, remove from BBQ or smoker. Slice thinly and cook as you would any bacon.

Note: Your bacon will keep for a couple of weeks refrigerated. Any longer and you should slice, vacuum seal and freeze. After you have cured your first batch of bacon, you can adjust the amount of salt and sugar to your liking. You can even add maple syrup if you wish but do not adjust the amount of curing salt. If you like your bacon on the savoury side, you could add other ingredients to your cure such as fresh ground black pepper, bay leaves or garlic.

Curing salt is important in the curing of meat. Most importantly, it prevents bacteria from growing, most notably botulism. It is a mixture of salt (93.75%) and sodium nitrite (6.25%). It's what gives ham or bacon its pinkish red colour and distinctive taste. Do not try to cure meat without it.

Cure for Hams

You can use this recipe to cure a whole hind leg of pork. Depending on the size of the leg of pork, you may need a five-gallon bucket to fit the leg. I have cured upwards of a 28-pound leg. You will need to make several batches of the brine to cover the leg. If you cure a whole leg, you should use an injector needle and inject the brine all over the leg so it cures from inside out, as well. It will help cure the leg quicker. You will need to refrigerate the leg in the brine. The rule of thumb is a day for every two pounds: I had to keep my 28-pounder in brine for two weeks. The next day, I smoked it for 24 hours using cherry wood. It was wonderful. You can use any hardwood you have on hand. I like to use either cherry, apple, oak or maple wood.

Weighing your salts and spices is more accurate than measuring by the spoonful. However, if you don't have a scale that measures in grams, I have included approximate measures by the spoonful. The recipe below is designed for you to cure a just a few pounds at a time. Have fun with it.

INGREDIENTS:

4 L water (about 16 cups)

350 g sea salt (about 1 ½ cups)

500 g - 1 kg light brown sugar (about 4-8 cups)

42 g pink curing salt* or cure #1 (2 ¾ T)

1 pork loin or a bunch of pork sirloins, upwards of 3 - 4 kg (7-9 pounds)

Add salt, sugar and pink salt to water. Stir often till water has absorbed all the ingredients. Cut loin into 1 kg pieces (about 2 pounds each) and add to chilled brine. Cover with a plate to keep hams submerged in brine. Brine for at least 48 hours, refrigerated. Preferably 3 days. Remove from brine and pat dry.

Place hams on a rack and let it dry for 4 - 6 hours refrigerated or overnight to form a pellicle. It should feel dry or tacky to the touch.

Now it's time to smoke and cook your hams.

Smoke on your smoker or you can use your BBQ. Smoke for about 2 - 3 hours depending on thickness. Preheat BBQ to about 250 degrees F.

If you don't have a smoker, no worries. Take a chunk of hardwood, wrap in foil, remove the grill and put directly on the burner of your BBQ. Poke a bunch of holes in the top of the foil to let the smoke escape. Turn burner to high. Turn most of your remaining burners off. Try to maintain around 250 degrees F in your smoker or BBQ.

When smoke appears, reduce the heat under your chunk of wood to about medium. Place your hams on a rack away from the heated side of your BBQ and smoke using indirect heat. Let it smoke for between 2 and 3 hours, checking occasionally and turning your hams from time to time.

Check internal temperature at the 2 hour mark. You are looking for an internal temperature of 150 degrees F.

Enjoy.

Curing salt is important in the curing of meat. Most importantly, it prevents bacteria from growing, most notably botulism. It is a mixture of salt (93.75%) and sodium nitrite (6.25%). It's what gives your ham or bacon its pinkish red colour and distinctive taste. Do not try to cure meat without it.

Cure for Peameal Bacon

St. Lawrence Market in downtown Toronto is known for its peameal bacon sandwiches. With this recipe, you can save the travel, and look no further than your own kitchen to enjoy a great peameal bacon sandwich! It's more accurate to weigh your salts and spices than to measure them by the spoonful. However, if you don't have a scale that measures in grams, I have included approximate measures by the spoonful or cup.

INGREDIENTS:

4 L water (about 16 cups)
300 g sea salt (about 1 ½ cups)
400 g brown sugar (about 1 ¾ cups)
42 g pink curing salt* or cure # 1 (about 2 ¾ T)
7 bay leaves
2 T pickling spice

5 - 6 garlic cloves, smashed with the side of your knife
1 full pork loin (maximum of 4 kg, about 9 pounds)
Cornmeal

Add salt, sugar, pink salt, bay leaves, pickling spice, and garlic to water. Stir often till water has absorbed all the ingredients. Chill brine.

Cut loin into 1 kg pieces (about 2 pounds) and add to chilled brine. Cover with a plate to keep submerged in brine. Brine for up to three days (at least 48 hours), refrigerated. Remove from brine and pat dry.

Roll your cured loins in cornmeal. Wrap tightly in plastic wrap. It makes it easier to slice. Slice according to your preference. I like mine on the thicker side, about ¼-inch thick. Thinner slices are better if you are making peameal sandwiches.

Your peameal bacon will last for a week to 10 days in the refrigerator. Any longer and you should slice and freeze in serving-size portions.

Curing salt is important in the curing of meat. Most importantly, it prevents bacteria from growing, most notably botulism. It is a mixture of salt (93.75%) and sodium nitrite (6.25%). It's what gives your ham or bacon its pinkish red colour and distinctive taste. Do not try to cure meat without it.

Cure for Salt Beef

This cure can be used to create a brine/pickle for any meat product. Here in Newfoundland, salt beef is the typical salted product used in a traditional Jiggs' dinner. The salt meat is generally watered out overnight, then boiled for about two hours. Then copious amounts of root vegetables and cabbage are cooked for another 40 - 50 minutes. Now you have a Jiggs' dinner. You can also use this brine to pickle pork riblets, baby back ribs, pork hocks, tongues or even moose ribs. It's more accurate to weigh your salts and spices than to measure them by the spoonful. However, if you don't have a scale that measures in grams, I have included approximate measures by the spoonful/cup.

INGREDIENTS:

4 litres water (about 16 cups)

1.2 kg sea salt (almost 5 cups)

100 g white sugar (about ½ cup)

60 g pink curing salt* (4 T)

Mix all ingredients together in a plastic bucket, sized 2.5 gallons or larger. Stir a few times till salts and sugar are dissolved.

Use 3 kg (6-7 pounds) of beef navel or whatever meat you are planning to pickle. Cover with cold water for an hour or two to remove some of the blood before putting it in your brine.

Drain beef and add to brine. Refrigerate for 2 weeks. Your beef is now fully cured. Keep refrigerated and use within 3 - 4 months. Alternatively, remove from brine, vacuum seal and freeze for use later.

*Curing salt is important in the curing of meat. Most importantly, it prevents bacteria from growing, most notably botulism. It is a mixture of salt (93.75%) and sodium nitrite (6.25%). It's what gives your salt beef its red colour and distinctive taste. Do not try to cure meat without it. Do not use pink Himalayan salt, it's not the same.

Tasso Ham

Dave, this one's for you.

As with my other cure recipes, I find that it's more accurate to weigh salts and spices than to measure them by the spoonful. However, if you don't have a scale that measures in grams, I have included approximate measures by the spoonful/cup.

BASIC CURE:

450 g fine sea salt (almost 2 cups)
250 g sugar (white or brown, your preference) (1 cup)

60 g pink curing salt (4T)
Mix all ingredients and store in air tight container

Depending on how you plan to use the tasso ham, you can pretty well use any cut of pork for this recipe. Just keep in mind the thicker the pieces, the longer time for the cure to take. I have used pork shoulder cut into about 1-inch thick slices. When fully cured and cooked, I chop it into smaller pieces for my gumbo. I have also used sirloins, full loins and even tenderloins. Tenderloins work wonderfully if you want to add the ham to a charcuterie board. They slice easily and present well on your board along with other charcuterie selections.

For this recipe, I am suggesting you use pork loins or tenderloins. A 2 kg (4 ½ lb.) piece of pork loin or use 4 pork tenderloins, about 1.5 kg (about 3 1/2 lb.) total weight.

If using the loin or tenderloin, remove the silver skin before placing in the cure.

If using the loin, start by removing the silver skin. Now, cut the loin in half, into 2 pieces about 1 kg (about two lb.) each. Now cut each loin into 3 equal pieces lengthwise. You should have 6 strips of pork about 6 inches long each and a bit more than an inch thick. If using the tenderloin, just remove the silver skin and leave whole.

These will be cured using the salt box method. Using a flat-bottom glass dish or non-reactive dish add about ½ cup of the basic cure to bowl. Rub each piece of pork on all sides to absorb as much cure as will stick to the pork, shaking off any excess. Continue adding as much dry cure to the bowl as you need to ensure all sides of your pork get an even coating of cure. Wrap bowl with cling film and refrigerate for about 5 - 6 hours, turning occasionally. Let it sit overnight if you are not in a rush to try it. You will notice the pork giving up some of its liquid, which is natural. Pork will firm up to the touch. Cure has now done its job.

Remove from brine, rinse under cold water and pat dry. Now it's time to rub your pork with the spice rub and smoke your tasso hams.

DRY SPICE RUB FOR TASSO HAM:

5 T fresh ground black pepper

2 T garlic powder

1 T onion powder

1 T smoked paprika

1 T dry thyme leaves

1 t allspice powder

2 t cayenne powder

Mix dry ingredients together. You may need to adjust the amount of cayenne powder to suit your taste. Place your mini tasso hams in a bowl. Shake about ½ of dry rub over the hams and rub in to ensure all sides are covered with the rub. Shake off excess or add more as needed. You have enough dry rub here to spice about 8 tenderloins or approximately 3 kg (6 ½ lb.) worth.

Now it's time to smoke your hams.

Smoke on your smoker or you can use your BBQ. Smoke for about an hour depending on thickness. Preheat BBQ to about 300 degrees F. If you don't have a smoking unit, no worries. Take a piece of hardwood, wrap in foil and put directly on burner of your BBQ. Poke a bunch of holes in the top of the foil to let the smoke escape. Turn burner to high. Turn off all remaining burners. When smoke appears, place your tasso hams on rear rack of BBQ on indirect heat. Let smoke for 45 min to 1 hour, checking occasionally and turning hams from time to time.

Check internal temperature at the 45 minute mark. You are looking for an internal temperature of 150 degrees F. Remove from BBQ and let rest for 20 minutes. Slice thinly. Or if using in a gumbo, store till required. Then cut into small ½-inch pieces.

Smoked Chicken and Roasted Garlic Sausage

These sausages are sooo good. Once you make them, they will become a regular in your household. I have a little pork mixed in with the chicken thighs. However, if pork is not a part of your diet, just replace it with more chicken thighs. Don't be afraid to increase the amount of roasted garlic too if you are a garlic fiend. I like to stuff the sausage into hog casing. However, you can use collagen casings if you wish.

Yields: about 20 six-inch sausages
Preheat oven: 350 degrees

INGREDIENTS:

3 lb. of boneless skinless chicken thighs, diced
2 lb. of pork shoulder, diced
Drizzle olive oil
2 heads garlic, oven roasted
1 T dried thyme (1 T)
55 g fine sea salt (2 T)
6 g pink curing salt* (1 t)

10 g fresh ground black pepper (1 T)
1 g cayenne powder (¼ t)
¼ cup olive oil
4 large onions, peeled and chopped
10 feet of hog casing, washed and soaked
in cold water for about 30 minutes

Peel away most of the papery outer layers from the garlic. Cut a little slice off the top of each head of garlic to expose the cloves. Lay out a piece of foil wrap large enough to wrap the garlic. Lay garlic on foil wrap and drizzle with a little olive oil. Wrap to close foil and bake for about an hour till soft.

Remove from oven and let cool a little. Remove cloves from the head and squeeze the cloves from the bottom to remove the garlic. Set aside the garlic to process with the onions.

Meanwhile, heat oil on medium heat and sauté onions for 20 - 25 minutes till caramelized. Add caramelized onion along with the roasted garlic to a food processor and pulverize till smooth. Add a few tablespoons of white wine if necessary to achieve a smooth consistency.

Remove from food processor to a small bowl and place in refrigerator to cool.

Grind your chicken thighs and pork shoulder using the medium die of your meat grinder into a large bowl. Add your caramelized onion and garlic mixture, your thyme, both salts, black pepper and cayenne powder. Mix everything together until well mixed.

If you don't have a meat grinder, chop your meats in a food processor.

Fry a little piece of your sausage to check for seasoning. Adjust if necessary.

Stuff the sausage into your casings. Twist at 6-inch intervals. Twist every other sausage in the opposite direction.

Now it's time to smoke your sausages. Keep your sausages linked together to smoke.

You can either use your smoker or your BBQ. Smoke for about an hour or two till cooked. Preheat smoker or BBQ to about 200 degrees F. If you don't have a smoking unit, no worries. Take a chunk of hardwood, wrap in foil, remove the grill and put directly on burner of your BBQ. Poke a bunch of holes in the top of the foil to let the smoke escape. Turn burner to high. Turn off most of your remaining burners.

When smoke appears, reduce heat to about medium under the chunk of wood. Place your sausages on the smoker or, using indirect heat on the BBQ, to smoke for about 2 hours. Check sausages occasionally and move about to ensure even smoking.

Check internal temperature of the sausages at the one-hour mark. You are looking for an internal temperature of 160 degrees F. When reached, remove from BBQ or smoker and enjoy.

Note: *For leftovers, reheat your sausages using medium heat on the BBQ or just pop them in a 300 degree F oven for 15 minutes.*

*Curing salt is important in the curing of meat. Most importantly, it prevents bacteria from growing, most notably botulism. It is a mixture of salt (93.75%) and sodium nitrite (6.25%). It's what gives ham or bacon its red colour and distinctive taste. Do not try to cure meat without it.

Cajun Boudin (Sausages)

The Cajun boudin is a type of sausage traditionally made with a mixture of ground pork, liver, rice and seasonings. Its history dates back two centuries or more to the Acadians who migrated to Louisiana from Nova Scotia, so there is a nice connection to Atlantic Canada here. There are many versions of boudin, ranging from very mild to hot. This one I make here is considered a white boudin. There is also a red version, so called because of the addition of pork blood along with the ground pork, liver, rice and seasonings.

My brother Bud spends a lot of time in the US, especially in the Texas and Louisiana area. He has eaten his share of boudin. On his last visit here in Newfoundland we created this recipe together, taking the best ideas from a bunch of other recipes and improving from the previous batches we had made in the past. We both like them spicy, so we have a fair amount of cayenne powder and jalapeños. Feel free to reduce the amount if you wish.

Yields: approximately 50 four-inch sausages (boudins)

INGREDIENTS:

10 lb. pork shoulder

2 lb. chicken livers or pork liver, sliced

6 lb. onions, peeled and coarsely chopped

3 bunches green onions, white parts separated from the green tops

6 jalapeños, seeds removed, finely chopped

5 T sea salt

7 bay leaves

4 T cayenne powder

3 cups uncooked long grain rice

20 feet of natural hog casing

1 T salt reserved for poaching the boudin

Cut pork in long strips about 1 inch square and 5 - 6 inches long. Place in pot big enough to fit the pork, barely cover with cold water. Add sea salt, bay leaves and cayenne powder. Bring to boil, cover, reduce heat to simmer and cook until tender, about 90 minutes. Add liver and cook for an additional 10 minutes. Remove pork and liver with slotted spoon. Set aside to cool.

Add chopped onions and white parts of green onions to stockpot and cook on low heat for 20 minutes uncovered. Add jalapeños and cook for an additional 5 minutes. Using a slotted spoon, remove onions and peppers to a bowl to cool.

Reduce stock to 7 ½ cups. Add rice, cover and simmer for 20 minutes until rice is cooked and all the stock is absorbed. This should yield about 5 pounds of cooked rice. While rice is cooking, finely chop the green onions. When rice is cooked, remove cover and set aside to cool.

Now it's time to grind the pork, liver, onions, jalapeños and finely chopped green onions. Mix everything together in a large bowl. Set a large pan or bowl underneath your grinder and use a coarse grinder plate. Grind your pork strips, liver, onions, jalapeños, and finely chopped green onions. Add cooked and cooled rice to ground mixture and mix together. Taste and adjust seasoning.

Bring a large pot of water almost to a boil and add 1 T of salt. You'll use this to poach your sausages.

Rinse and soak about 20 feet of natural hog casings. Using a sausage stuffer, stuff mixture loosely into casing. Twist or tie into sausages every 4 inches or so. When you start twisting the sausages, twist every other sausage in the opposite direction.

To poach the sausages, you want the water simmering at no more than 175 degrees F. Gently put sausages in water and poach for 10 minutes, keeping the temperature of the water between 165 - 175 degrees F.

If you wish, you can smoke some of the sausages now at 200 degrees F or less for an hour or so after poaching.

Although the boudins are now ready to eat, they are better if baked in an oven at 350 degrees for 20 minutes or so.

After enjoying them over the course of a few days for breakfast, I will normally vacuum seal the rest in batches of 3 or 4 for the freezer, where they're good for several months.

Polish Kielbasa with Ham

Kielbasa is Polish for sausage. There are numerous types of Polish sausages. For this one, I use pork. The ground pork is emulsified by adding ice and milk powder and beating it for about 5 minutes in a stand mixer with a paddle. I love kielbasa with ham. So, for this sausage, I have added small cubes of my own cured and smoked ham just before stuffing into the casings (see page 176). If pork is not part of your diet, this sausage can easily be made from beef and omit the ham. If using beef, ensure you add between 20 and 30% beef suet. Remove any fat and sinew, then grind the beef cubes and suet together. Weighing your salts and spices is more accurate than measuring by the spoonful. However, if you don't have a scale that measures in grams, I have included approximate measures by the spoonful.

Yields: about five 24-inch-long kielbasas

INGREDIENTS:

10 lb. of pork shoulder, diced and chilled

1 ½ lb. of smoked ham, cut in ½-in. dice or smaller (reserved till you are ready to stuff into the casings)

120 g fine sea salt (5 T)

14 g pink curing salt* (2 ½ t)

50 g white sugar (4 T)

28 g fresh ground black pepper (3 T)

28 g dry mustard (4 T)

12 g garlic powder (1 T)

4 g dried marjoram (2 T)

1 g cayenne powder (½ t)

140 g dry milk powder (1 cup)

6 cups of crushed ice

18 - 20 feet of large beef casings, about 2 in. in diameter, washed and soaked in cold water for about half an hour

Grind the pork shoulder using the large die of your meat grinder. Partially freeze. Remove from freezer, mix in both salts, sugar and crushed ice and grind again, this time using the small die of your grinder.

Add black pepper, mustard, garlic powder, marjoram, and cayenne powder and mix till well incorporated. Separate into 4 batches.

Working in batches, add the first quarter of the pork mixture to the bowl of a stand mixer. Using paddle attachment beat at high speed for 3 - 4 minutes. Add ¼ cup of milk powder and continue to beat for a couple of minutes till mixture is homogeneous. Repeat for the next 3 batches.

Now bring all 4 batches together and mix again. Add ham cubes and mix together. Now it's time to stuff your casings. Using the largest funnel you have, stuff your sausage into your casings.

Normally we twist our sausages in about 6-inch lengths. This time, because the casing is so large, we will leave them without twisting and tie them in about 18 - 24 inch lengths.

Now it's time to smoke and cook your kielbasa. This is normally done by smoking at a low heat and cooking it at the same time. You need to smoke with hardwood. My preferences include cherry, apple, oak and maple wood.

You can either use a smoker or a BBQ. Place your sausages on the smoker or use indirect heat on a BBQ to smoke for about 2 - 3 hours till cooked. Check sausages occasionally and move about to ensure even smoking. Check internal temperature of the sausages at the 2 hour mark. You are looking for an internal temperature of 150 degrees F.

If you're using your BBQ, preheat to about 200 degrees F. Take a chunk of hardwood, wrap in foil, remove the grill and put directly on burner of your BBQ. Poke a bunch of holes in the top of the foil to let the smoke escape. Turn burner to high. Turn off most of your remaining burners. When smoke appears, reduce heat to about medium under the chunk of wood. You may need to turn on a second burner to maintain your 200 degrees F. Place your sausages on the smoker or on a rack on your BBQ on indirect heat to smoke for about 2 - 3 hours. Check sausages occasionally and move about to ensure even smoking.

Check internal temperature of the sausages at the 2 hour mark. You are looking for an internal temperature of 150 degrees F. When done remove from BBQ or smoker and enjoy.

Curing salt is important in the curing of meat. Most importantly, it prevents bacteria from growing, most notably botulism. It is a mixture of salt (93.75%) and sodium nitrite (6.25%). It's what gives ham or bacon its pinkish red colour and distinctive taste. Do not try to cure meat without it.

Irish Blood Pudding

The word blood connotes yuckiness, especially when someone tells you to eat it. But believe you me, these puddings/sausages are a staple in any good Irish breakfast and many a Newfoundlander's breakfast. If you can put aside your queasiness and try these puddings, you will become a convert very quickly. It's not easy to find pork blood these days. However, if you make friends with a local butcher in your neck of the woods, you can be sure they can source it for you. I like to use larger beef middles to form the puddings, so while you are at the butcher ask them for some beef casings, too.

INGREDIENTS:

1 stick butter
3 lb. onions, peeled and finely chopped
2 cups beef suet
12 cups breadcrumbs (or Newfoundland
    Purity factory hard tack, crushed fine)
4 cups pork blood
2 large eggs, beaten
1 T fresh ground black pepper
3 T salt

½ t cayenne powder
½ t ground allspice
¼ t ground cloves
1 T thyme
1 t oregano
1 t paprika
25 feet of beef casings, approximately
    1.5 in. in diameter

Heat butter on medium heat in a sauté pan, add onions and sauté for 8 - 10 minutes till soft and translucent. Transfer onions to a large bowl. If you can find the hard tack, ensure you crush them. If you have pieces the size of a pea, don't worry about it. Add the remaining ingredients except the beef casings. Stir until well blended.

Now it's time to make your puddings. I like to use a larger size beef casing, approximately 1.5 inches in diameter.

However, you could actually bake the pudding in glass loaf pans if you choose. If you go this route, bake them in a preheated 300 degree oven in a bain-marie (also known as a water bath or double boiler) for 1 - 1 ½ hours until firm to the touch. Before baking, cover the pans with foil wrap to prevent the puddings from drying out.

If you want the traditional method, use the beef casings. Set up your sausage stuffer using the large funnel. Oil the funnel with a little vegetable oil and slide the beef casing on over the funnel. Start stuffing your casing tying or twisting them every 5 - 6 inches, or whatever size you like. Use a pin to burst any air bubbles in your sausage. Now you are ready to poach.

Bring a large pot of water almost to a boil. Temperature should be no more than 190 degrees F. Put the sausages in the 190 degree F water. The temperature will immediately fall. Poach for 25 - 30 minutes till firm to the touch while trying to maintain roughly 170 degrees F.

Do not let the water come to a boil. Your puddings will burst open. Your puddings are done when firm to the touch or the internal temperature of your puddings are 150 degrees F, then remove from the pot and let cool.

The best way to serve these puddings is to slice them into thin slices, about ½ inch thick. Pan-fry till crispy on both sides. Enjoy as part of your own Irish or Newfoundland breakfast.

Pork Breakfast Sausage

This sausage recipe can be stuffed into pork casings if you have them, but it works equally well when flattened out as patties. Either way this recipe will yield about a dozen 4 ounce sausages or sixteen 3 ounce ones. Use what you need and freeze the rest. If making patties, freeze uncooked patties with a piece of wax paper or parchment paper between each patty. I love these for breakfast.

INGREDIENTS:

3 lb. ground pork
½ cup ice cold water
1 T fine sea salt
1 t fresh ground black pepper
1 T ground sage

½ t ground allspice
½ t garlic powder
2 t onion powder
1 t paprika
¼ t cayenne powder

Put ground pork in a mixing bowl. Mix all seasonings together in a bowl. Sprinkle over ground pork. Add ice water. Using your hands, mix well to incorporate the spices and the water into the pork.

Stuff into casings or flatten into patties. If making patties, keep them less than ½ thick. Use your thumb to put an indentation in the centre. This will help keep them flat and prevent them from forming into a ball.

Add a little oil to a frying pan and pan-fry on medium heat till done, about 3 - 4 minutes per side.

International Dishes

Chicken Tikka Masala

In Indian restaurants, chicken is normally baked in a tandoori oven. I don't have one, so I cook mine over direct heat on the BBQ. This recipe has two steps: making the chicken tikka and then the masala. First we make the chicken tikka by marinating and partially cooking the chicken. The second step is to make the masala, a tomato cream sauce in which the chicken tikka is finished. I suggest chicken breasts here as my wife is fond of them. Me, not so much. I prefer chicken thighs. However, this is one recipe where I don't mind the breast meat. The marinade helps keep the chicken moist.

CHICKEN TIKKA INGREDIENTS:

2 lb. boneless skinless chicken
   breasts or chicken thighs
1 cup plain yogurt
4 T olive oil
5 T lemon juice, freshly squeezed
4 large cloves garlic, finely chopped
3 T fresh ginger, grated

1 t turmeric
2 T garam masala
1 T ground coriander
1 T Kashmiri chili powder or paprika
1 t fresh ground black pepper
1 t fine sea salt

Cut each chicken breast into 5 - 6 pieces. If using chicken thighs, leave them whole. Set aside. Mix remaining ingredients together in a large bowl. Add chicken pieces. Cover with the marinade and let sit in the refrigerator overnight or at least an hour or two.

Preheat BBQ to highest setting. Stir the marinade and grill the chicken pieces 3 - 4 minutes per side to get nice grill marks on them. Normally the chicken is skewered before cooking it. I don't bother. After cooking, set aside. Chicken is not fully cooked at this stage. You will finish it later in the masala sauce.

MASALA INGREDIENTS:

4 T ghee or vegetable oil
2 small onions peeled, cut in half
   top to bottom, finely sliced
2 large cloves garlic, finely chopped
2 T grated fresh ginger
1 T garam masala
1 T ground coriander

1 t ground cardamom
½ t cayenne powder (optional)
1 t fine sea salt
1 cup tomato sauce
1½ cups heavy cream (35%)
2 sweet bell peppers, cut into 2-in. sq. pieces

Heat ghee or oil in a Dutch oven. Add sliced onion and cook 5 - 6 minutes until soft. Add garlic and ginger, stir and cook for another minute. Add dry spices and cook for another minute or so stirring constantly. Stir in salt, tomato sauce and heavy cream.

Let simmer for a few minutes. Add chicken and bell peppers and let simmer for 12 - 15 minutes covered. Serve with basmati rice and naan.

Pushpa's Chicken Curry

This is the first curry dish I ever made. A friend of mine at work came from India and he and his wife taught me how to make it. It seems like I have made it a thousand times. It's a really simple dish and I hope you will enjoy it for many years like I have. Thanks, Pushpa.

INGREDIENTS:

1 whole chicken, cut into pieces,
   or about 3 lb. of chicken
4 T ghee or ¼ cup olive oil
1 T black mustard seeds
3 medium onions, finely chopped
4 garlic cloves, finely chopped
3 T fresh ginger, grated
1 T curry powder

1 t coriander powder
1 t cumin powder
1 finely chopped Habanero (optional)
1 (28 oz.) can tomatoes (reserve
   2 tomatoes for the rice)
2 t salt
1 t fresh ground black pepper
5 bay leaves

Heat ghee or oil in heavy-bottom pot on medium-high heat. Add black mustard seeds and cook for about one minute, stirring constantly. As soon as they start to pop, add the onions. Cook for about three minutes.

Now add the garlic, ginger, curry powder, coriander powder and cumin powder and cook for another couple of minutes, stirring constantly. Now add the Habanero and can of tomatoes. Gently crush the tomatoes.

Remember to keep aside the two tomatoes reserved for the rice. Add the chicken pieces, salt, pepper and bay leaves. Stir to incorporate everything.

Reduce heat to low, cover and cook for one hour, stirring occasionally till chicken is cooked through.

Remove cover for last 10 - 15 minutes of cooking time to let sauce thicken a little.

Serve with basmati rice (see my recipe on page 201) and naan.

Hint: This dish works equally well with cubes of beef or lamb. If you like spicy food, this is a dish that can handle heat. Chop and add as much of your favourite chilies early on and let them spice up your dish. Mango chutney works well with this dish, too.

Indian Lamb Curry

I love lamb. One day I was watching a cooking show, and saw an Indian chef cooking a lamb shank curry using Kashmiri chilies. I was inspired and immediately ordered Kashmiri chilies online. When they arrived I created this lamb curry. Kashmiri chillies are somewhat mild and add a very bright red hue to your curry. If you can't find them, use five parts of mild paprika to one part cayenne powder. My brother Bud loves this dish.

Serves: 8

INGREDIENTS:

3 lb. of lamb, cut into 1-in. cubes
1 cup full-fat plain yogurt
1 T Kashmiri chili powder

1 T turmeric powder
3 T ginger, freshly grated
3 T garlic, finely chopped

Mix yogurt and spices together in a large bowl. Add lamb and mix well. Place in refrigerator to marinate for a couple of hours, preferably overnight.

Now it's time to make the tomato gravy and get the lamb cooking.

INGREDIENTS:

¼ cup edible mustard seed oil or ghee
10 whole cloves
1 T cardamom seeds
2 - 3 pieces whole cinnamon, depending on size
7 bay leaves
4 cups chopped onions
1 T turmeric powder

2 T coriander powder
1 T cumin powder
2 T Kashmiri chili powder*
3 t salt
1 (28 oz.) can fire-roasted tomatoes
1 t fish sauce
1 cup water

Preheat pot on medium-high heat. Heat up the mustard seed oil and add cloves, cardamom seeds, cinnamon and bay leaves. Stir to bring out the flavours for a few minutes.

Now add the onions and sauté for 10 - 15 minutes till soft. Add the remaining spices and salt, sauté for a couple of minutes. Add tomatoes and fish sauce, stir and let simmer for a few minutes. Add lamb and stir.

Increase heat and bring to a boil. Reduce heat to low and let simmer uncovered for 10 minutes adding water as necessary to prevent lamb from sticking.

Continue to simmer on low heat for about 2 hours, covered for the first hour or so, then uncovered till tender and the sauce has thickened a little, or bake in a preheated 325 degree F oven for about 2 hours uncovered till tender. You want to sauce to be thick not watery.

Enjoy with your favourite basmati rice and naan.

Note: If you want to use bone-in chicken, I would make the sauce and cook it for about 20 minutes before adding the chicken. Cook the chicken for about an hour till tender.

*Substitute 5 teaspoons mild paprika and 1 teaspoon of cayenne if you can't find Kashmiri chili powder. Add more cayenne if you like your curry hotter.

Basmati Rice

Basmati rice is a long-grain slender rice grown in and around India and Pakistan. It's a simple but great tasting rice to serve with any of your favourite curries. Try one of my curries in this book if you're feeling adventurous.

INGREDIENTS:

1 cup basmati rice
1 ¾ cups chicken stock or water
1 t salt
4 T ghee

1 t cumin seed
2 canned tomatoes, chopped
      (reserved from your curry)

Put rice in a bowl. Cover with water and swirl your hand in the water to dislodge the starch molecules. The water should be cloudy now. Rinse and repeat till the water is clear. Let the rice sit covered in water for 10 minutes. Drain.

In a medium saucepan, heat ghee on medium heat. Add cumin seeds and stir till lightly toasted. Do not leave unattended as they will burn. Now add drained rice, salt and chicken stock or water and chopped tomatoes to pan. Stir, bring pot to a boil, then cover and reduce to its lowest setting for 15 minutes undisturbed.

Turn off heat and let sit for 5 minutes. Fluff with a fork and serve with your favourite curry.

Indian Basmati Rice and Lentils

I sometimes make this dish by itself without making a curry. I loved taking it to the office and reheating it for breakfast or lunch. It's so good.

INGREDIENTS:

½ cup dried green lentils (soaked in
 boiling water for at least 1 hour)
1 cup basmati rice, washed and rinsed
5 T ghee or oil
1 t black mustard seeds
1 whole cinnamon stick
3 bay leaves
3 whole cloves
1 t cumin seeds
1 t red pepper flakes

1 medium onion, finely chopped
2 t fresh garlic, chopped
2 t fresh ginger root, minced
2 t turmeric powder
1 t coriander powder
1 t cardamom powder
¼ t cayenne powder
2 t salt
3 cups no-salt chicken stock

Put rice in a bowl. Cover with water and swirl your hand in the water to dislodge the starch molecules. The water should be cloudy now. Rinse and repeat until the water is clear. Let the rice sit covered in water for 10 minutes. Drain.

Heat a saucepan on medium-high, and add ghee until hot. Now sauté whole spices in ghee until fragrant, 2 - 3 minutes.

Add onion and sauté for about 5 minutes till softened. Then, add the garlic, ginger and remaining dry spices. Stir for another couple of minutes to help bring out the flavours.

Now add the drained lentils and the rice. Add stock, stir and simmer covered for 15 minutes. Remove from heat and let sit for at least 5 minutes to finish steaming the rice. Fluff with a fork. Remove any of the whole spices you see and discard. Serve as is, or with your favourite curry.

Spicy Thai Chicken and Shrimp

I love spicy food. I cooked a spicy crab dish following a recipe years ago. I wanted to make it again using shrimp instead of crab, but I couldn't find the recipe. I remembered some of the ingredients, so this is what I ended up making instead. It's sweet, salty, spicy and sour all at the same time. My friend Danny loves heat and scotch as much as I do (well, almost as much), so any time he comes by for supper, I make a version of this dish for him. Hope you try it.

Serves: 4 - 6

INGREDIENTS:

¼ cup peanut oil

2 onions, coarsely chopped

1 lb. boneless chicken thighs, cut
    into small thin pieces

3 T garlic, freshly chopped

¼ cup ginger, freshly grated

3 T lemongrass, very finely
    chopped (or from a jar)

¼ cup cider vinegar

¼ cup fish sauce

3 T brown sugar

2 hot peppers, finely chopped
    (I use Habaneros)

2 red bell peppers, chopped into
    pieces roughly 1-in. sq. pieces

½ cup white wine or chicken stock

1 lb. raw shrimp, peeled and
    deveined (shells reserved)

½ cup chopped green onions

2 cups uncooked Thai sticky rice

Cook rice according to package instructions and set aside.

In small saucepan, add shrimp shells and wine. Bring to a boil and turn off. Let shells poach in the wine while you bring the dish together. Set aside.

Heat a wok on high, then add the peanut oil. Next add your onions and sauté for a couple of minutes. Next add the chicken and sauté for about a minute, just to brown a little.

Now add garlic, ginger, lemongrass and sauté for another minute. Then add the vinegar, fish sauce, sugar, hot peppers, and chopped red bell peppers.

Stir to bring all ingredients together for a minute. Add strained stock and shrimp. Let cook for 3 - 4 minutes. Taste for seasoning. Add salt or more heat as required.

Add chopped green onions and serve on a bed of Thai sticky rice.

Thai Drunken Noodles

This particular dish was made famous by Chef Jet Tila while he was a chef in Las Vegas. It's a dish made all over Thailand and like most famous dishes, there are many versions. Here is mine.

Serves: 4

INGREDIENTS:

8 oz. wide Thai noodles soaked in hot water according to package directions and drained. Set aside.

FOR THE SAUCE:

¼ cup hot water

1 T brown sugar

2 T chicken concentrate

2 T soy sauce

2 T fish sauce

3 T oyster sauce

3 T chili paste

3 T mirin (sweet rice wine)

1 cup chopped Thai basil

Mix all ingredients together except the basil. Set aside.

FOR THE CHICKEN:

¼ cup peanut oil

½ lb. boneless chicken breasts
   or thighs, thinly sliced

1 medium onion, sliced very thinly

3 cloves garlic, finely chopped

1 Habanero, finely chopped

1 sweet pepper, cored and cut in thin strips

4 baby bok choy, quartered

Heat a wok on high heat for a minute. Add half the peanut oil. When hot, add chicken and sauté for a minute. Remove chicken from wok and set aside.

Add the remaining peanut oil, then add your onion, garlic, Habaneros and peppers and cook for a minute or so. Add bok choy and stir for another minute or so. Add your sauce and bring to a boil. Return your chicken and the drained noodles to the wok, and stir till the noodles have absorbed the sauce.

Stir in the chopped basil. Serve and enjoy.

Thai Curry

This is a quick and easy recipe that takes about 30 minutes to prepare. I use a store-bought curry paste: you can choose between a yellow version (mildest), red (medium) or green (the hottest). Depending on the brand, these pastes generally contain garlic, ginger, lemongrass, galangal, shrimp paste, kaffir lime leaves, chilies and other spices that can be difficult to find: hence the reason to use ready-made. For the rest of the recipe, you can use any combination of ingredients you like. I like to use onions, sweet peppers, mushrooms, carrots and snow peas or sugar snap peas if I can find them. For the protein, I generally use chicken thighs and shrimp. Alternatives include thinly sliced pork, baby corn, eggplant, baby bok choy, asparagus, zucchini, etc.—whatever vegetables you enjoy. If using eggplant, try to find the skinny purple ones that are sometimes labelled Japanese or Chinese eggplant.

INGREDIENTS:

4 T canola oil or any neutral oil

4 - 5 T Thai curry paste

2 onions, peeled and cut in thin slices vertically
    top to bottom (looks nicer than chopped)

2 cloves garlic, finely chopped

1 lb. boneless chicken thighs, cut
    into small pieces or thinly sliced
    chicken breasts if you prefer

1 cup mushrooms, sliced

1 (14 oz.) can coconut milk

1 T fish sauce

1 large carrot, sliced or grated

1 sweet pepper, coarsely chopped

1 cup snow peas

1 lb. shrimp, shelled and deveined

½ cup Thai basil leaves (optional)

In small saucepan, add shrimp shells to the coconut milk. Bring to a boil and turn off. Let shells poach in the coconut milk. Set aside. (When ready to use, remove and discard shrimp shells.)

Heat oil in a wok or heavy-bottom pot. Add curry paste and cook for about 1 minute stirring constantly.

Stir in onion, garlic, chicken and mushrooms. Cook for a couple of minutes stirring occasionally. Add strained coconut milk. Bring to a boil. Reduce heat, cover and simmer for 5 minutes.

Now add remaining ingredients except snow peas and shrimp. Cover and simmer for an additional 10 minutes. Add snow peas and shrimp. Simmer for an additional 3 - 4 minutes. Top with the fresh basil. Serve with jasmine rice.

Easy Mexican Chicken Lasagna

One evening at the condo in Toronto, my wife and I couldn't decide what to have for dinner. We both love Mexican but we didn't have enough of anything to make one of our traditional dishes, so we created this recipe. The tortillas would be best toasted on an open fire. If you have a gas stovetop, toast them on one of your burners.

Preheat oven: 400 degrees (convection if you have it)

INGREDIENTS:

1 ½ lb. of boneless skinless chicken thighs, cooked and shredded (you can also buy a roasted chicken and shred that)

2 cups water

2 t salt

2 large potatoes peeled and thinly sliced

¼ cup olive oil

2 large onions finely chopped (about 2 cups)

2 sweet peppers, seeded and chopped

4 cloves garlic, finely chopped

1 T smoked paprika

½ t cumin

¼ t cayenne pepper

1 t fish sauce (optional)

1 (430 ml) jar spicy tomatillo sauce

12 corn tortillas

2 cups Monterey Jack cheese, grated. You could also use old cheddar, or a combination of whatever cheeses you have.

Bring water and salt to a boil in a pot. Add chicken, return to a boil and reduce to a medium-low simmer for about 20 minutes. Remove chicken with a slotted spoon to a plate to cool. Reserve water. Peel and slice potatoes thinly, about ¼-in. thick. Add to reserved chicken water and boil potatoes for about 10 minutes. Remove with slotted spoon. Bring water back to a boil to reduce to about half a cup. Reserve.

Heat a deep-sided frying pan on medium high. Add olive oil, onions and peppers. Sauté while stirring for about 5 minutes. Add garlic, cook an additional 2 minutes.

Add spices, fish sauce, shredded chicken, and reserved water. Bring back to a boil to bring all ingredients together. Pan should be almost dry at this point. If not, simmer till almost all the water has evaporated.

Now it's time to bring the casserole together. Start by spreading ¼ jar of tomatillo salsa on bottom of a 14-in. x 9-in. casserole dish. Start layering: tortillas, potatoes, salsa and cheese. Do 3 layers. Finish with a layer of cheese.

Bake on preheated 425 degree convection oven for 20 minutes till cheese is melted and starting to brown nicely.

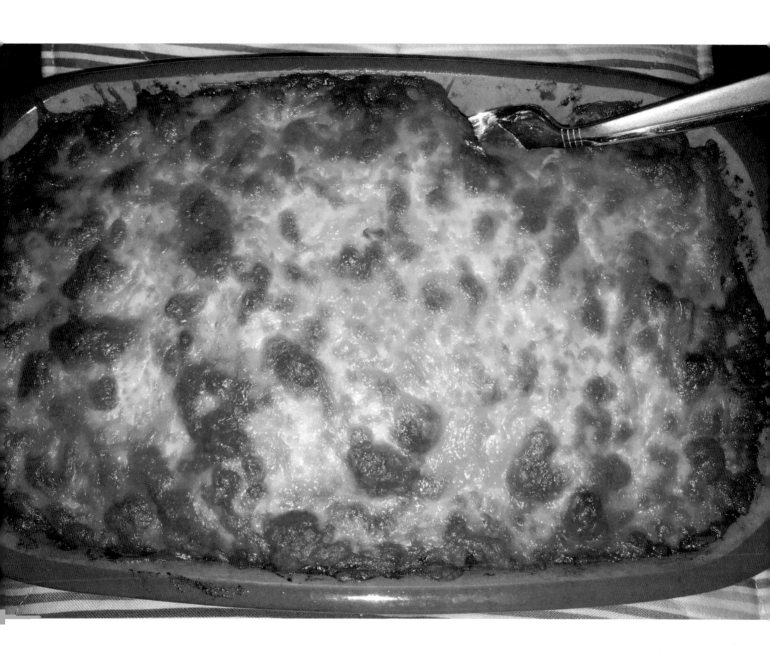

Barbacoa Burritos

This is a simple Mexican dish. To save time you can use ground meat, but the small cubes of beef and pork make the texture worth the time to cut them. Just mix everything together and pop it in the oven. Serve with Mexican red rice. Feel free to add some fresh jalapeños.

Preheat oven: 400 degrees

INGREDIENTS:

2 lb. pork shoulder, cut in ½-in. cubes
1 lb. beef, cut in ½-in. cubes
1 large onion, finely chopped
1 (425 ml) bottle BBQ sauce,
 approximately 1 ¾ cups
1 T cumin powder
1 T onion powder
1 T garlic powder

2 t salt
½ t fresh ground black pepper
1 t chipotle chili powder (or
 regular chili powder)
2 fresh jalapeños, finely chopped (optional)
1 t fish sauce (optional)
1 package of flour tortillas

Mix all ingredients together in an ovenproof dish or pot. Bake uncovered in a preheated 400 degree oven for 2 hours. Stir occasionally. You want a nice thick sauce. Wrap tortillas in foil and warm in the oven.

However, if you have a gas stove, toast the tortillas on the open flame instead, turning every few seconds to warm them and get some nice char marks. Fill with barbacoa and roll the tortilla. Serve with Mexican red rice.

Note: For a healthier version, add some chopped green peppers and a can of drained pinto beans with the rest of the ingredients and bake together.

Easy Chicken Enchiladas

This dish has become one of my family's regular menu items. We often will make large batches of our own enchilada sauce and bottle it or freeze it, making it a quick but delicious meal. I have included the recipe for our enchilada sauce on page 216, as it really makes a difference. But you can still enjoy this recipe with a can of store-bought enchilada sauce.

Serves: 4
Preheat oven: 400 degrees

INGREDIENTS:

1 rotisserie chicken, meat removed and
    shredded (or poach 4 chicken breasts
    in chicken stock, then shred)
2 Spanish onions, peeled cut in half and sliced
2 red or other sweet bell peppers, sliced
3 cloves garlic, finely chopped
1 t dried oregano
1 t cumin powder

½ t cayenne powder
1 t salt
1 t fish sauce (optional)
½ cup white wine
8 medium tortillas
1 (10 oz.) can enchilada sauce
12 oz. shredded Tex-Mex blend of
    cheese (or your favourite cheese)

In deep frying pan on medium heat, add olive oil and sauté onions for about 5 minutes. Add peppers and garlic and continue to sauté for a few more minutes. Stir in chicken, white wine, 2 tablespoons of the enchilada sauce and remaining spices to pan. Cook uncovered for about 10 minutes till pan is almost dry.

Spread about ¼ can of enchilada sauce in baking dish. Divide enchilada mixture evenly between the 8 tortillas. Roll each tortilla, placing seam-side down in dish.

Once all your tortillas are filled, spoon remaining enchilada sauce over the top and then cover with shredded cheese. I like to use lots of cheese, but cover with the amount you feel comfortable with.

Bake for 30 minutes in a preheated 400 degree oven. Let rest for 5 minutes before you serve.

Enchilada Sauce

Making your own enchilada sauce will make a world of difference to your enchiladas. It will be nothing like the canned stuff that is made mostly from tomatoes with very few chiles. I try to include a selection of chiles: any combination of what I have on hand or can buy at the time. This may include dried anchos, mulatos, pasillas, chipotles, moritas, chiles de árbol, or guajillas. Generally, I use a bunch of each and make a batch that I bottle off in small jars for future use. All peppers have different heat levels. Generally, the smaller the pepper, the hotter. If you want a milder sauce, use more anchos and guajillas than any others. Here are the chiles I used for the last batch I made.

Yields: about a dozen 125 ml jars

INGREDIENTS:

20 ancho chiles
30 guajillo chiles
10 chile de arbol (hot)
5 chipotle peppers (sometimes hot)
6 small onions, peeled and cut in half

10 - 12 cloves garlic
2 cups chicken stock
6 T brown sugar
1 T fish sauce (optional)

Start your sauce by heating a cast-iron pan on medium-high heat. Add the chilies and toast for a few minutes. You will notice the colour change and you will smell the aroma. You will need to toast them in batches. Remove from the pan to a deep bowl and let cool. Tear open the chiles and remove and discard the stem and the seeds. Put the chiles back in your deep bowl.

Now cover them with about 2 cups of boiling water. You will need to weigh them down with another bowl or plate. Let sit for a minimum of 30 minutes in the boiling water. Now start adding the chiles to a blender along with the onions and garlic. Pour the soaking liquid in the blender and pulverize along with the chiles.

It took me three batches to get them all pulverized. Add a little boiling water if necessary to get them pulverized. The sauce should be a thick soupy sauce at this point.

Pour into a heavy-bottom pot and bring to an easy simmer. Be careful as the sauce will start to spit very quickly. You want it on the lowest setting, with the cover on the pot. Add the chicken stock, sugar and fish sauce. Simmer for about an hour on low heat, stirring often. Taste and add a touch of salt if necessary.

You can either process in small jars or freeze in small sandwich bags for future uses. You will use about a cup of enchilada sauce per batch of enchiladas. This recipe should yield about 8 cups of enchilada sauce.

Hint: I have also used a can of chipotle peppers in adobo sauce in combination with the dried chilies. Be careful as they can be very hot. You could even add a bunch of fresh tomatoes if you have them on hand.

Huevos Rancheros

Any time I travel, I am always looking for something interesting for breakfast besides the standard fare. One Saturday morning I wanted to make one of these interesting breakfasts for myself, and this was the result. It's much better than most of the breakfasts I have tried elsewhere. I hope you give it a try.

Serves: 4

INGREDIENTS:

2 T olive oil
1 lb. ground pork
1 onion, finely chopped
2 cloves garlic, finely chopped
1 t cumin powder
1 t smoked or regular paprika
½ t Mexican or regular oregano
½ t chili flakes (or to your preference)

1 t salt
½ t fresh ground black pepper
1 cup boiling water
4 tortillas, toasted
4 eggs, poached
8 oz. queso fresco or smoked
    cheddar cheese, shredded
Salsa to serve

Heat oil in heavy pan on medium heat. Add onions and sauté till soft, about 2 - 3 minutes. Add pork breaking up and stirring till lightly browned, about 8 - 10 min. Add chopped garlic, cumin, paprika, oregano, chili flakes, salt and pepper to combine. Add water, stir and cover till most of the water is evaporated.

Meanwhile, toast your tortillas. If you have a gas stove top, laying your tortilla directly on the burner for a few seconds, turning often, or place under your broiler till toasted to your liking. Next poach your eggs and prepare to plate.

Preheat broiler to high. Set rack about 6 inches below your broiler.

On an ovenproof plate, add a toasted tortilla, ¼ of pork mixture and poached egg, and cover with ¼ of cheese. Prepare remaining plates. Broil till cheese is melted, then top with salsa and serve.

Note: Options are to add two poached eggs, a dollop of refried beans and/or a piece of avocado.

Moussaka

Moussaka is one of the more popular dishes of Greece. There are countless versions of moussaka made all over the Middle East, so you can experiment a bit. For mine, I use eggplant, potatoes and ground lamb and top it with a thick béchamel sauce. If you don't like eggplant or can't find it, use zucchini. The last time I made it, COVID-19 was rampant and my grocery store had no eggplant so we used zucchini from our garden.

Serves: 8

INGREDIENTS:

2 lb. ground lamb
4 onions, finely chopped
4 cloves garlic, finely chopped
2 cups tomato sauce
1 cup red wine
1 t fish sauce
2 t dried oregano
1 t ground cinnamon
1 t ground nutmeg

1 t ground allspice
¼ t cayenne
2 t salt
½ t fresh ground black pepper
1 large eggplant
4 medium potatoes, peeled and
    sliced in ¼-in. slices
Salt and pepper

FOR THE MEAT SAUCE:

Heat a heavy-bottom pot on medium-high heat. Add lamb and cook for about 10 minutes to brown the meat. Add chopped onions and cook for about 5 minutes. Add garlic and cook for a few more minutes. Add red wine and simmer till reduced in half. Add fish sauce, tomato sauce, oregano, cinnamon, nutmeg, allspice, cayenne, salt and pepper. Stir and cover.

Let simmer for 30 - 40 minutes. Depending on the grind of the lamb, there may be fat floating on the top. If so, try to spoon it off and discard.

EGGPLANT AND POTATOES:

Using a vegetable peeler, peel 5 - 6 strips lengthwise off your eggplant every two inches or so leaving a 1-inch strip of skin between what is removed. Slice in ¼-inch slices. Place sliced eggplant in a bowl, shallow pan or colander and sprinkle with salt. Let sit for about an hour. The salt helps remove some of the moisture and bitterness.

Now rinse the salt off the eggplant and pat dry with paper towel. Add a little olive oil to pan and cook the eggplant in batches 3 - 4 minutes per side to brown. Remove to paper-lined sheet pan.

Peel potatoes and slice into ¼-in slices. Add oil to pan and fry potatoes in batches 3 - 4 minutes per side till lightly browned and partially cooked. Remove from pan and set aside on sheet pan with the eggplant.

BÉCHAMEL INGREDIENTS:

1 stick butter
½ cup all-purpose flour
½ t nutmeg, grated
Pinch of cayenne
3 cups whole milk

1 cup Parmigiano-Reggiano or
    Pecorino Romano, grated
Salt and white pepper to taste
3 egg yolks
½ cup Parmigiano-Reggiano,
    grated for the top

Melt butter on medium-high heat in a heavy-bottom pot. Now add flour, stirring constantly to incorporate all the flour into the butter. Slowly whisk in the milk, a little at a time, continuing to whisk. When sauce starts to bubble it's time to stir in the cheese. Add salt and white pepper to taste. Let cool slightly. Stir in egg yolks. Set aside.

Now it's time to pull together the moussaka.

Arrange all the potatoes slices in a greased 9-in. x 13-in. casserole dish. Top potatoes with half the meat sauce.

Next, layer the eggplant followed by the remaining meat sauce. Top with the béchamel sauce, spreading evenly across the top. Top with the remaining cheese.

Bake in a preheated oven on 350 degree convection or 375 degree regular heat for one hour till bubbling and browned on top. Serve with a salad and crusty bread.

Open-Face Jerk Chicken Sandwich with Collard Greens

I have been eating jerk chicken on bread for years. However, one evening as I was cooking the chicken on the BBQ, I found a bowl of cooked kale and collard greens in the fridge. I used this as a base for my sandwich and have been making the greens for this open-face sandwich ever since. There are all kinds of jerk seasoning mixes available today in all supermarkets. I like to use the Walkerswood brand when I am too lazy to make my own. It's always consistent. See page 224 for my jerk seasoning recipe.

Serves: 4

INGREDIENTS:

4 crusty rolls, cut in half
8 boneless skinless chicken thighs
2 T olive oil
1 T soy sauce
2 - 3 T jerk seasoning, depending
    on how hot you like it
3 T olive oil
5 slices of bacon, chopped
2 bunches collard greens (thick stems
    removed and discarded) or kale
    and chopped into 2 in pieces

1 large Bermuda onion, finely
    chopped (or 2 regular onions)
3 cloves garlic, finely chopped
½ cup white wine
1½ cups chicken stock
2 T cider vinegar
1 t fish sauce
¼ t cayenne pepper (optional)
Salt and fresh ground black pepper

Mix the olive oil, soy sauce and the jerk seasoning together in a bowl. Add chicken thighs and rub in the marinade. Let sit overnight or at least an hour to infuse the chicken with the jerk flavour.

Heat olive oil in a large heavy-bottom pot over medium-high heat. Add bacon and cook until crisp. Remove bacon from pan and reserve. Add onion, and cook until tender, about 5 minutes. Add garlic, and cook for a further 2 minutes. Add collard greens, and fry until they start to wilt. Add white wine, chicken stock and vinegar. Bring to a simmer. Add remaining ingredients and season with salt and pepper.

Reduce heat to low, cover, and simmer for 45 minutes, or until greens are tender. Keep an eye while cooking as the broth will steam away. Ideally, there will be very little broth remaining when greens are cooked. Add reserved bacon and check for seasoning.

Preheat BBQ to high. Cook marinated chicken thighs 10 - 12 minutes depending on thickness till done. Leave thighs whole or chop into smaller pieces. Brush cut side of rolls with olive oil and toast on BBQ for a few minutes. Alternatively, broil bread till toasted, just a minute or so.

Place greens on roll and top with chicken thigh. Serve.

Jamaican Jerk Seasoning

I love Jamaican jerk chicken with collard greens on a toasted bun. Once you try it, you will be hooked too. This jerk seasoning will last forever refrigerated. Start with less heat if you wish. You can always add more. It should taste hotter by itself as you will be adding it to flavour your food. Use this seasoning on pork, chicken or fish. I hope you enjoy it as much as I do.

INGREDIENTS:

3 - 4 bunches green onions, coarsely chopped
4 - 6 whole Scotch bonnets or Habaneros,
    stems removed and discarded
½ cup whole allspice berries, toasted
1 T fine sea salt

3 whole nutmeg, toasted
2 T fresh ground black pepper
2 T dried thyme leaves
1 cup dark brown sugar

Heat a small cast-iron pan on medium heat for 4 - 5 minutes. Dry-roast the whole allspice berries and the nutmeg in your heated cast-iron pan for a couple of minutes till you start to smell them. Shake pan often to ensure the spices get toasted evenly.

Remove and grind your allspice berries and toasted nutmeg into a fine powder using a spice grinder or a coffee grinder.

Cut green onions into 1-inch pieces. Add onions and all the remaining ingredients to the bowl of your food processor including your ground allspice and nutmeg. Pulse until everything is combined into a smooth paste. Feel free to increase or decrease the amount of Scotch bonnets to suit your taste.

Pour the jerk marinade into a jar and keep refrigerated.

When you're ready to use it, add a few heaping tablespoons of your jerk marinade in a bowl. Add a couple of tablespoons of oil and a tablespoon of soy sauce. Mix together.

Add a pound of your favourite pork or chicken pieces. Stir to cover your meat in the jerk marinade and let sit anywhere from 60 minutes to overnight to develop the flavours. Grill on medium to medium-high heat till cooked. Enjoy.

Cuban Chicken BBQ

Cuba is one of my favourite destinations. It's got everything we need: sun, sand, rum and cigars. One evening, the resort we stayed at had a beach BBQ where they served a delicious garlicky-citrusy chicken. Here is my take on this wonderful chicken dish.

Preheat BBQ: 300 degrees

INGREDIENTS:

1 whole chicken (about 4 lb.), or use chicken pieces

FOR THE MARINADE:

½ cup melted butter or olive oil

Zest of 1 lime

½ cup orange juice

½ cup fresh lime juice

½ cup sherry

8 large cloves garlic, finely chopped

2 t dried oregano

1 t ground cumin

¼ t cayenne powder

1 t fresh ground black pepper

2 t fine sea salt

½ t white sugar

1 T fish sauce (optional)

Spatchcock the chicken. Yes, it's a real term that means "to flatten," and it's a way to cook the chicken by removing the back bone and flattening the chicken out. Start by laying the chicken, breast side down on your cutting board. The legs should be pointing away from you. The goal here is to remove the backbone.

Take a pair of poultry shears and cut straight down one side of the neck bone all the way to the tail. Now start on the other side of the neck bone and cut straight to the tail again. You will have removed a bone about 2 inches wide and about 6 - 8 long. Discard or save for stock later. Don't forget to clean your shears when you're done this part.

Now turn the chicken breast side up and push the breast down with the heel of your hand. This will help release the breast bone and allow you to flatten out the chicken. Next, cut a shallow incision into each thigh and drumstick. Do the same in the thicker part of the breast. This will help the marinade permeate the chicken.

Gather together all your ingredients for the marinade. Mix all ingredients together in a large bowl. Place spatchcocked chicken in the marinade. Let sit overnight in the refrigerator or at least for a few hours. Bring to room temperature for an hour before grilling.

Place chicken skin side up on preheated BBQ. Cook for 30 - 35 minutes. Flip over and cook for another 10 minutes or so till done. Insert an instant-read thermometer into the thickest part of the breast. Chicken is cooked at 160 degrees F. Let rest for 10 minutes, then serve with your favourite sides.

Portuguese Salt Fish
(Bacalhau à Gomes de Sá)

My friends JP and Elizabeth visit Portugal twice a year. I have been very fortunate to have travelled with them to experience the wonderful cuisine Portugal offers. We love going to "hole in the wall" restaurants as they truly offer the best of Portuguese cuisine. Portugal and Newfoundland have a lot in common. Years ago, the Portuguese White Fleet sailed to the Grand Banks of Newfoundland to fish for the bountiful cod fish. The Portuguese fishermen rowed away from the mother ship in a dory to jig for cod for the day. The catch was brought back, split and salted aboard the mother ships. Today, salt cod (bacalhau) is still a big part of the Portuguese diet. It's been said that Portugal has 365 ways to cook bacalhau. I don't doubt it for a minute as I have eaten many of them. Here is one of them. It's a popular and very simple dish of salt cod, potatoes, onions, black olives, olive oil and hard boiled eggs.

Preheat oven: 350 degrees

INGREDIENTS:

1 lb. salt fish, watered
1 lb. potatoes, peeled and cut into ½-in. slices
2 lb. onions, peeled and sliced
½ cup olive oil
1 large clove garlic, crushed

1 cup black olives, pitted
Fresh ground black pepper
Extra olive oil to drizzle on top
3 hard-boiled eggs, peeled and
   thickly sliced or quartered

Cut salt cod into pieces. Place in a large bowl and cover with cold water. Change water 2 - 3 times over a 24-hour period.

Two pounds of onions seems like a lot and it is but they really shrink up when caramelized. Add onions to sauté pan with the olive oil.

Cook on medium heat for about 20 - 25 minutes till onions are browned and caramelized. About halfway through, add the garlic and continue cooking onions. You may need to add a little more oil or butter to prevent onions from burning. Set aside and keep warm.

While onions are caramelizing, bring a pot of cold water to a boil. Add cod and bring back to a boil. Simmer for about 5 minutes. Remove cod to a large plate. Remove skin and bones from cod and discard. Try not to break up the cod too much. Set aside cod and keep warm.

Meanwhile, add potatoes to pot and bring back to a boil. You just want enough water to barely cover the potatoes. Reduce heat to medium and cook potatoes till almost cooked.

Now it's time to bring everything together. In a casserole dish, add potatoes, cod and black olives. Add a little fresh ground black pepper. Cover with the caramelized onions and olive oil. Drizzle a little extra olive oil over everything.

Pop your dish in the oven for 30 - 35 minutes. Remove from the oven and top with the quartered eggs. Serve.

Grilled Calf's Liver Portuguese-Style

On our last trip to Portugal, we drove to a restaurant in the mountains. There was no menu and it was easy to see why. It was an open-air restaurant owned by a couple who owned a butcher shop, grew their own vegetables and raised their own cattle. I can still see how they hung their onions from rafters of the restaurant to dry, which they also grilled, whole and unpeeled. Their main offering was beef, grilled over an open fire, including the liver and heart. I love liver but had never dreamed of grilling it. What a surprise! It was sliced thin, brushed with a little olive oil from their garden, just a touch of piri piri hot sauce and a little salt and pepper. Grilled over an open fire for just a minute on each side, it was heaven on a plate. Here is my version and if you like liver, I am sure you will love this version too.

Serves: 4

INGREDIENTS:

2 lb. calf's liver, sliced thinly

4 T olive oil

1 T piri piri hot sauce

Salt and fresh ground black pepper to taste

Wash and dry liver. In a medium bowl, add olive oil and piri piri hot sauce and whisk together. Add liver and turn to coat both sides of each slice in the oil mixture. Let sit till grill is ready.

Prepare a charcoal grill: when the coals turn white, you are ready to grill. Make sure your grill is clean. If you don't have a charcoal grill, your propane grill will suffice. Just get it hot.

Before you start grilling, move the liver slices around in the bowl to ensure you get a good coating of olive oil on each side. When it's all laid out on the grill, touch it with a little salt and pepper. Grill for about 1 minute or so per side depending on thickness.

Remove from grill and serve with your favourite vegetables.

Note: If you can't find piri piri, use a teaspoon of your favourite hot sauce. Piri piri sauce isn't all that hot.

Asian BBQ Ribs

If you're running short of time, you can speed things up a little by baking these ribs in a covered roasting pan at 325 degrees for about two hours. This can be done a day in advance. Add ¾ cup of boiling water to the pan, cover and bake. When ready to serve, grill on indirect heat for 30 - 40 minutes, basting a few times.

Serves: 6 - 8
Preheat BBQ: 300 degrees

INGREDIENTS:

3 racks of baby back ribs

MARINADE:

⅔ cup hoisin sauce	2 T sesame oil
⅓ cup plum sauce	2 T Chinese Shaoxing wine or dry sherry
¼ cup oyster sauce	2 T rice wine vinegar
¼ cup soy sauce	1 T orange rind, grated
¼ cup honey	¼ t cayenne powder
2 T fresh ginger, grated	1 T Chinese five-spice powder
3 cloves garlic, finely chopped	1 ziplock bag

You should remove the membrane to help the marinade penetrate the ribs. Place ribs meat-side down on a cutting board. Remove the membrane from the back of the ribs by gently inserting a butter knife between a bone and the membrane. Pick a bone in the middle. Be gentle and wiggle the knife. Get your finger between bone and the membrane. Work your finger down the bone and eventually get a second one in there. Pull membrane off. Discard. Cut ribs into 2 pieces.

Mix all marinade ingredients together. Put prepared ribs in a ziplock bag. Add marinade and rub into the ribs. Let sit for a few hours or overnight in the refrigerator, turning occasionally.

Remove ribs from bag. Pour marinade into a small saucepan. Bring to a boil and turn off heat. Use to brush on ribs. BBQ on indirect heat for approximately 2 ½ - 3 hours on a medium flame till tender. Try to maintain about 300 degrees F. Baste occasionally. Serve with your favourite sides.

Cambodian Ribs

Ribs are always a crowd favourite and there are thousands of different versions to try. I encourage you to experiment using different spices, rubs and sauces. Here is a recipe that I created that is non-traditional but delicious.

Serves: 4
Preheat BBQ: 300 degrees F

INGREDIENTS:

2 racks of baby back ribs

FOR THE MARINADE:

4 T brown sugar
1 T onion powder
½ t cayenne powder
4 T fish sauce
4 T fresh lemongrass, very finely
    chopped or use a bottled version
Juice of 1 lemon
2 T hot sauce

2 T soy sauce
2 T oil
1 t salt
1 t black pepper
4 T fresh ginger, grated
4 T garlic, finely chopped
1 ziplock bag

Mix all ingredients for the marinade together. Set aside while you prepare the ribs.

To prepare ribs, remove the membrane on the back of the ribs. Place ribs, meat-side down, on a cutting board. Remove the membrane from the back of the ribs by gently inserting a butter knife between a bone and the membrane. Pick a bone in the middle. Be gentle and wiggle the knife. Get your finger between the bone and the membrane. Work your finger down the bone and eventually get a second finger in there. Pull membrane off and discard.

Marinate the 2 sides of baby back ribs. Cut ribs in half, place in a large ziplock bag and pour in the marinade, place in refrigerator for a few hours or overnight.

Preheat BBQ to about 300 degrees F.

For the best results, BBQ on indirect heat for approximately 2 - 3 hours. Serve along with your favourite sides.

Haggis

Haggis is the national dish of Scotland. The dish is a big part of Robbie Burns night, traditionally piped in on a fancy platter and served along with copious amounts of Scotch (or should I say drams). If made in the traditional way, lamb heart, liver and the lungs are cooked along with oatmeal, onions, suet and spices in a sheep's stomach. These days, lungs are a banned substance, so instead, I use a mix of lamb hearts, liver, kidneys and tongues along with ground lamb and beef. Go easy on the liver: two pounds is more than enough. For my picture here, I have shown a couple of my mini haggises. If you wish, you can remove the haggis from the casing to serve it alongside mashed turnip or rutabaga and potatoes or "neeps and tatties" as the Scottish would say.

Yields: about forty 6-inch mini haggises

INGREDIENTS:

5 lb. lamb offal (heart, liver, kidneys, tongue)

3 T sea salt

7 bay leaves

2 cups steel cut oats, toasted

1 lb. beef suet, ground

2 lb. ground lamb

2 lb. ground beef

3 lb. onions, peeled and finely chopped

5 cloves garlic, finely chopped

2 T fresh ground black pepper

1 t cayenne powder

4 T marjoram

1 T nutmeg, freshly grated

2 T thyme

6 cups lamb stock (reserved from cooking the offal)

1 large dram of Scotch

1 T sea salt reserved for poaching the haggis

25 - 30 feet of beef middles (casings)

You'll also need a meat grinder or food processor.

Cover the offal with cold water and bring to a boil. Add the salt and the bay leaves. Reduce heat, cover and simmer for 2 hours until the meat is tender. Remove the offal from the pot and let cool. Discard bay leaves. Reduce stock to 6 cups and set aside.

Preheat oven to 400 degrees. When heated, lightly toast oats for about 10 minutes. Set aside.

When your offal has cooled, get it ready to grind. Cut away the ventricles on the hearts. Peel the tongues. Now cut the meat into strips and pass through the coarse grinding plate of your grinder. Grind your suet along with the meats to incorporate well. Collect your grindings in a big bowl or pan large enough to hold all your ingredients.

Pan-fry ground lamb and beef till browned, about 15 minutes. Remove ground lamb and beef and add to ground heart and liver mixture, draining any fat back in the pan. Add the onions to the pan and cook on medium heat for about 6 - 7 minutes.

You are not looking to brown the onions, just cook them till soft. Add garlic and cook for another minute or so. Add the toasted oats and 2 cups of the reserved lamb stock. Stir to allow the oats to soak up the stock. When the stock is all absorbed, add to the meat mixture.

Measure your spices and add to your pan with the meat and onion mixture. Stir well to incorporate. Add the scotch to the remaining 4 cups of stock. Add the stock to the pan with the ground meat mixture and mix well. Now you are ready to stuff your casings.

Set up your sausage stuffer and attach your 1-inch horn. Lightly oil your horn and slide about 10 feet of casing over the horn. Tie a knot in the end.

Now you are ready to start stuffing the casing. Remember to fill the casing no more than two-thirds full. You need space for the oats to swell. You can either twist or tie them every 6 inches or so.

Heat a large pot of cold water to about 190 degrees F. Add a tablespoon of sea salt. Add all your mini haggises to the pot. Poach for 3 hours.

The temperature will fall to about 150 degrees F after adding the haggises. Increase heat till the temperature comes up to 170 degrees F. Then reduce heat to minimum. Try to maintain 170 - 175 degrees F for 3 hours. Don't let the water come to a boil, as you risk bursting your casings.

Remove your haggises from the pot and enjoy with neeps and tatties (mashed turnips and mashed potatoes). To reheat, I like to bake mine in a 300 degree F oven for about 20 minutes.

Note: The five pounds of lamb innards will be reduced to a little over two pounds when cooked. The four pounds of ground lamb and beef will yield a little over three when cooked. In total, you will have about five-and-a-half pounds of cooked meats. Since sheep's stomachs are very hard to come by, I use beef middles. You will need about 25 - 30 feet. I twist mine into roughly 6-inch lengths. Twist every other sausage/haggis in the opposite direction.

Easy Korean Cod

I had some fresh cod a few years ago and wanted to cook it differently than I had cooked it before. This is the dish I created. It's so easy to pull together. I hope you like it.

Serves: 2

INGREDIENTS:

2 fresh cod loins (about 8 oz. each)
3 T olive oil

FOR THE MARINADE:

1 t sesame oil
1 T soy sauce
1 t fresh ginger, ground

1 t garlic, finely chopped
½ t fine sea salt
1 T gochujang paste

Mix together the marinade ingredients in a bowl. Add cod and marinate overnight.

Preheat oven to 350 degrees.

Heat a cast-iron pan on medium-high heat. Add olive oil. Place cod on hot pan and pop in the oven for about 10 minutes till done and fish flakes easily. Serve with oven roasted potatoes and green beans sautéed in garlic for a few minutes or on a bed of your favourite rice.

Curry Mix for Chicken Wings

This is a great curry powder mix to shake on your food and cook on your BBQ. Use on chicken wings or boneless skinless chicken thighs. My sister Yvonne and her daughter Ashley use it on boneless skinless chicken breasts, too.

Yields: about 3 cups

INGREDIENTS:

2 cups Madras curry powder (or
    similar curry powder)
2 T garlic powder
2 T onion powder
1 T cayenne powder
1 T cumin powder

1 T coriander powder
1 T cardamom powder
1 T smoked paprika (or regular paprika)
5 T salt
4 T sugar
2 T fresh ground black pepper

Mix all ingredients together and store in a jar with a lid.

For a great finger food before dinner, use 2 pounds of chicken wings separated, saving the tips for stock. Put wings in a bag or bowl. Add ¼ cup of curry powder and shake to cover. Add more if necessary. Grill on top rack of medium hot BBQ for 25 - 30 minutes till done. Turn often to prevent burning.

Note: you can adjust any of these seasonings to your taste the second time you make it.

Spanish Tortilla

This is a classic Spanish tapa eaten throughout Spain. Using a minimum of ingredients, it really tastes delicious. I don't think I held a party in recent memory where my friend Danny didn't bring a big plate of tortillas and every time the plate was cleaned. Thanks, Danny, for your friendship and for helping me with the many charity dinners we cooked together.

INGREDIENTS:

1 ½ lb. of yellow potato, peeled
    and thinly sliced (¼ inch)
8 oz. dry cured chorizo, very thinly sliced
2 medium Spanish onions, peeled
    and thinly sliced

5 T olive oil
6 large eggs, beaten
Salt and pepper

Heat a heavy 10-inch non-stick frying pan and lightly fry chorizo until just browned. Remove chorizo from pan and wipe out the pan with paper towel.

Heat 3 tablespoons of olive oil in the same frying pan. Add potato, onion and few good pinches salt and pepper to taste to the pan. Cook over medium-low heat until tender, about 20 minutes, stirring occasionally. Remove from pan and allow to cool for 10 minutes. Wipe out the pan with paper towel again.

Add the cooled potato, onions and chorizo to the egg mixture. Add a little salt and pepper to the egg mixture. Stir to combine.

Heat the remaining 2 tablespoons of oil in the pan on low heat and pour the potato egg mixture into the pan. Cook for 10 - 15 minutes until the mixture is set. While cooking, use a flexible spatula to loosen mixture from the sides and shake pan to prevent sticking.

Place a large plate upside down over the pan and quickly flip the pan over to invert the tortilla onto the plate. Slide the tortilla back into the pan. Gently fry until the tortilla has completely set. Remove from pan and cut into small bite-size pieces. Use plenty of toothpicks to pass around. Enjoy warm or at room temperature.

One-Offs

Pastry for Stew

By adding this pastry to an already-cooked favourite stew, like the chicken stew found on page 78, you'll take your meal over the top. No one will go to bed hungry with this meal for supper.

Preheat oven: 375 degrees

INGREDIENTS:

2 cups flour, plus a little additional
    flour for the board
4 t baking powder
2 eggs, beaten

⅔ cup cold whole milk
Good pinch of salt
1 stick cold butter, chopped

The key to a good tender pastry is handling it as little as possible. Start by adding flour, baking powder and salt together in a bowl. Mix ingredients. Chop butter in pea-size pieces. Rub into flour. Add milk to beaten eggs and add to dry ingredients. Barely mix the pastry.

Dump out on a lightly flour dusted board. Fold over pastry no more than 12 times. Flatten out pastry to about ¾-inch - 1-inch thick. Gently place on top of cooked stew and bake for 25 minutes at 375 degrees uncovered.

Remove from oven. Dish up your stew along with a piece of the pastry. If you make a rabbit stew, gently remove the pastry from the stew. Because the rabbit is on the bone, it's difficult to dish both the stew and the pastry together. Dish up the rabbit stew and serve with a piece of the pastry. Enjoy.

Chicken and Mushrooms with Stilton Cream Sauce

While my sister was away on vacation a few years ago, she had a wonderful chicken dish in a Stilton cream sauce. She asked if I could I make it for her. Having no idea how someone else made this dish, here is my take on her new-found favourite. The first time I made it, the sauce did not have the pungent flavour you would expect from Stilton. So, the next time I made it, I saved the rinds from a few chunks of Stilton. Bingo! You need the rind to get the Stilton flavour to really shine through. So if you like this recipe, start saving your Stilton rinds.

Serves: 4

INGREDIENTS:

4 boneless skinless chicken breasts

3 oz. Stilton

4 large portobello mushrooms

8 oz. oyster mushrooms

1 stick butter, cut in 2 pieces

Make a slit in the thick end of each chicken breast to make a deep pocket halfway through the breast. Stuff about a teaspoon or two of Stilton in each breast. Set aside to sear later. Now clean the portobellos. Pull away the stalk and save for another use. Take a spoon and scrape away the black gills. They are fine to eat, but I find that they add too much black colour to the dish.

Heat a fry pan to medium-high heat. Add ½ the butter and sauté the oyster mushrooms. Add a little salt and pepper. If the mushrooms are big, tear them in half. Cook until they have browned nicely and no water is left in the pan. Remove from heat and set aside.

Add remaining butter to pan and sauté the portobellos for about 5 minutes. While they are sautéing, stuff some of the oyster mushrooms in the slit of the chicken breast. This will add flavour to the breast meat and keep the Stilton inside. Move the portobellos to an ovenproof dish. Set aside.

Preheat oven to 400 degrees. Now sauté the breasts for about 4 - 5 minutes per side to get some nice colour. Place the breasts atop the portobellos and bake for about 20 minutes until the breasts are fully cooked. Internal temperature should read 160 on a thermometer.

Now it's time to make the béchamel sauce.

BÉCHAMEL SAUCE INGREDIENTS:

1 stick butter	1 cup whole milk
2 small onions, finely chopped	½ cup heavy cream
2 T flour	10 - 12 oz. Stilton cheese, including
Dash of cayenne powder	the rinds you saved
1 t Worcestershire sauce or fish sauce	½ t salt
¼ cup chicken stock	½ t fresh ground pepper

Melt butter on medium heat in a heavy-bottom pot. Add onions and sauté till just soft. You are not looking to fully cook them or even brown them, just get them soft. Now add flour and cayenne powder, stirring till flour is incorporated into the butter and onion mixture. Stir in the Worcestershire sauce, and chicken stock.

Now slowly whisk in the milk, a little at a time. Add cream and continue whisking. When sauce starts to bubble it's time to add your Stilton. Add salt and pepper as needed. Remove from heat and set aside.

Remove chicken from the oven when done. Plate the portobellos and chicken. Top with the Stilton cream sauce. Serve with your favourite vegetables or a rice pilaf.

Stuffed Roasted Saddle of Lamb

A few years ago I watched Chef Gordon Ramsay stuff a saddle of lamb, so when I bought my last whole lamb from Howard Morry, which I cut up myself, I set aside the saddle to stuff.

I know you can buy whole lambs at Costco cheaper but why not support your local farmers? I would rather buy local than buy one that's been frozen and shipped halfway around the world. Howie raises his sheep and lambs on an island in the Atlantic just off Ferryland called Isle aux Bois. His sheep and lambs spend their summers on the island enjoying the salty grasses. The New York Times wrote an article about Howie and his sheep a few years ago, saying his lambs were as good as those raised on the salt flats of France. If you're interested in reading more about this, I've included an article by Howie on my website www.corcorancooks.com: well worth a read!

Preheat oven: 350 degrees

Serves: 6 - 8

INGREDIENTS:
FOR THE LAMB:

1 saddle lamb, about 5 lb. deboned
   (net weight about 3 lb.)

Sea salt and pepper
2 T olive oil

FOR THE STUFFING:

4 T butter
½ lb. mixed wild mushrooms, chopped
1 medium onion, peeled and finely chopped
3 cloves garlic, finely chopped
3 T olive oil
3 cups cleaned turnip greens, kale
   or spinach, chopped

½ cup pine nuts, toasted
3 - 4 T mascarpone cheese
1 egg yolk
2 T fresh rosemary, very finely chopped
3 T Dijon mustard

FOR THE JUS:

1 cup port or sherry
2 cups lamb stock

Sea salt and fresh ground black pepper

Preheat oven to 350 degrees.

Debone saddle of lamb, set aside the fillets and save bones for lamb stock.

For the stuffing, heat butter in a cast-iron pan and sauté the mushrooms with a little salt and pepper until browned; drain in a colander sitting in a bowl to save juices for stock.

Now add the olive oil to the same pan. Add the chopped onion and sauté for 5 - 6 minutes. Then add the garlic and sauté for another minute. Now add the chopped greens and cook until just wilted. Add to the mushrooms.

After the mushrooms and turnip greens have drained, tip them into a bowl. Add the toasted pine nuts, mascarpone cheese, egg yolk, rosemary and a little salt and pepper. Mix into a paste and let chill.

Lay out saddle of lamb to prepare for stuffing. Rub saddle with Dijon mustard. Spoon the stuffing down the middle of the saddle. Cut the fillets horizontally (but not right through), open out and place over the stuffing. Fold one flap of the saddle over, then the other, wrapping firmly to make a neat roll. Tie with butchers twine in 4 - 5 places. Wrap in plastic wrap and chill for at least an hour.

Using the same cast-iron pan, heat a little olive oil on medium-high heat. Add a little salt and pepper on both sides of saddle. Place saddle back-side down. Brown for a few minutes, then turn the skin-side down and brown for a few more minutes.

Pop saddle in the oven and roast to 130 degrees F for medium rare, roast for about 45 - 50 minutes. Remove from oven and let rest on a plate tented with foil for about 20 minutes. It will gain between 5 and 10 degrees. Deglaze pan juices with port, add reserved mushroom juice and lamb stock, and reduce by half. Strain and adjust seasoning.

Serve the lamb thickly sliced, with the jus and your favourite vegetables.

Grilled Butterflied Leg of Lamb

My friend Terry came by for a visit today and brought a feed of fish and chips. We Newfoundlanders have some crazy sayings, and a "feed of fish and chips" is one of those sayings. Eating fish and chips is so good while you are eating it but sometimes it feels so bad an hour or so later because of all the grease. I digress. During his visit, Terry reminded me of a lamb dish I cooked for him and the crew on his sailboat about 15 years ago in Liscomb, Nova Scotia. We had engine problems, so while Terry and the boys fixed the engine, I prepared supper. He said it was one of the best meals he had ever eaten. I deboned a hind leg of lamb, and marinated it overnight with honey, port and copious amounts of fresh garlic and rosemary. Then we barbecued it. The honey actually chars the lamb. It looks burnt but it isn't, just charred. I forgot how good this leg of lamb was.

I once deboned five legs of lamb at about 2:00 a.m. after spending the night downtown. My brother-in-law Clarence was concerned I was going to cut off a finger or two. Not so, as it appears I can work just as well at 2:00 a.m. as 2:00 p.m. Here is the recipe for one leg. You can buy it deboned to save you time.

Preheat BBQ: 375 - 400 degrees

INGREDIENTS:

1 (7 - 8 lb.) hind leg of lamb, deboned and butterflied	1 bunch of rosemary, smashed to release the essential oils
¼ cup olive oil	1 T dried thyme
½ cup honey	1 T fine sea salt
8 cloves of garlic, finely chopped	1 t fresh ground black pepper
1 cup of port, sherry or red wine	1 ziplock bag

Combine olive oil, honey, garlic, port, rosemary, thyme, salt, and pepper in a bowl. Whisk everything together to ensure the honey is incorporated well. Now pour mixture into a large ziplock bag. Add lamb and seal bag, pressing out any air. Turn bag a few times to coat lamb in marinade. Refrigerate for at least 24 hours. Turn bag often to ensure marinade gets worked into the lamb.

Bring lamb to room temperature about 1 hour before grilling.

Grill lamb on direct heat for about 20 - 25 minutes. Lay lamb out flat on the grill. Turn the lamb a few times to ensure even cooking. Baste a couple of times with the marinade in the first 15 minutes.

Cook lamb until a meat thermometer inserted into the thickest piece of meat registers 120 - 125 degrees F for medium-rare meat.

Remove from the grill and let the lamb rest in a bowl to collect any juices. The thicker parts of the lamb are closer to rare right now.

However, you need to let the lamb rest for about 20 minutes. This will allow all the juices to remain in the meat not on your cutting board. By now the lamb will have gained about 10 degrees to medium, medium-rare. The thinner pieces will be well done. So you can satisfy everyone by taking it off the grill at 120 - 125 F and then letting it rest.

Now it's time to serve the lamb. Carve it by slanting your knife and cut slices across the grain and serve it with any juices accumulated in the bowl. After carving, sprinkle a little finishing salt on your sliced lamb like fleur de sel, or regular salt will do. Serve with roasted potatoes and grilled asparagus marinated in a little olive oil and balsamic vinegar. If you wish, serve alongside the tzatziki sauce.

TZATZIKI SAUCE:

1 cup cucumber, grated
1 ½ cups plain Greek yogurt (use your
    favourite)
2 T lemon juice
2 T olive oil
2 large cloves garlic, minced very fine
½ t fine sea salt
3 T fresh chopped dill (or mint if you prefer)
A good pinch or two of cayenne powder

Start by cutting your cucumber in half lengthwise. Using a spoon, scrape out the seeds and discard.

Now grate your cucumber. Then using a fine mesh sieve, squeeze as much water as you can from the cucumber. Add 1 cup of grated and drained cucumber to a bowl. Now add your remaining ingredients and stir.

Refrigerate overnight and serve with your grilled lamb.

Oven-Roasted Wild Partridge

If you are lucky enough to get your hands on wild partridge, this is an excellent way to prepare it. It's illegal to sell wild partridges, but no one said you can't pay someone to clean them for you. I hate cleaning them, so I get my brother-in-law Adrian to do it for me. I let him keep a few in return. It's one of my favourite meals.

Serves: 4
Preheat oven: 350 degrees

INGREDIENTS:

4 partridges, cleaned	4 T flour
Salt and fresh ground black pepper	A couple good dashes of cayenne powder
3 cups savoury chicken stuffing, see recipe on page 114	1 t fish sauce
	½ cup brandy or cognac
4 T olive oil	2 cups chicken stock
2 large onions, peeled and finely chopped	3 bay leaves
2 T butter	4 carrots, peeled, split in half lengthwise

Remove the liver, heart and lungs from the partridges and reserve. If the gizzards are included, remove them as well. Salt and pepper the cavity. Stuff the partridges with the stuffing. Using a long piece of string, tie the legs together. Then bring string up across the breast and down around the back and tie back to the legs. You may need to bring the string up one side and down the other to keep the legs and stuffing in place.

In a heavy-bottom pot large enough to fit the partridges, heat on medium-high heat. Add olive oil and brown the partridges, turning to brown evenly on all sides. Brown the heart, liver and gizzards for a couple of minutes. Remove along with the partridges to a plate.

Add onions and sauté 6 - 8 minutes till lightly browned. Add butter and flour and stir till incorporated. Add cayenne powder, a little salt and fresh ground black pepper, fish sauce and stir. Add brandy, chicken stock and bay leaves. Stir till the flour is incorporated well.

Lay carrots in bottom of pot. They will flavour the gravy and the keep the partridges up out of the gravy. You don't want the stuffing to get wet. Add back the heart, liver, lungs and gizzards. Now lay partridges atop the carrots.

Bake in preheated oven for about 2 hours till the partridges are tender. As these birds are wild game, they may be tough and may require more time.

I have cooked partridges many times. One or two can be tender and the others tough as nails. If so, remove the tender ones and continue baking the others till tender.

Remove partridges from pot and cut away the string. Serve one partridge per person along with the carrots and the heart, liver, lungs, gizzards and gravy. If you wish, you can cook potatoes in a separate pot to sop up the delicious gravy.

Salt Fish and Brewis

Salt fish and brewis was a staple in every Newfoundland kitchen. With the abundance of cod in our waters, we ate it fresh all summer long. The long cold winters brought dried salt cod to the table, along with another staple that had an indefinite shelf life—hard tack. Hard tack is made from only three ingredients: flour, water and salt. It's baked till it's dried out and hard. Hard as a rock some people would say. Many a tooth has been broken eating this stuff dry. To bring it back to life, it has to be soaked in liquid of some sort and then eaten. To make salt fish and brewis, the salt cod is watered for 24 hours or so, depending on how salty it is. The hard tack is soaked in water as well. It's all served with salt pork scrunchions and pan-fried onions. Scrunchions are made from salt pork fat back, cut into small pieces and fried till the fat is rendered out and the scrunchions remain. If the skin is left on the fat back and then cooked, you can hear you dinner companions scrunching on their salt pork; hence, the name. Boiled potatoes are sometimes added to round out the dish. Here is my take on salt fish and brewis.

Serves: 4 - 6

INGREDIENTS:

2 lb. salt cod	2 lb. onions, peeled and sliced or chopped
4 loaves hard tack	4 potatoes, peeled and cut into large chunks
8 - 10 oz. salt pork fat back	Fresh ground black pepper to taste

Cut salt cod into pieces. Place in a large bowl and cover with cold water. Change water 2 - 3 times over a 24-hour period. In a separate bowl, add hard tack. Barely cover with cold water and set aside for 24 hours as well.

Cut salt pork into very small pieces, about ¼-inch dice. Add to a sauté pan (we Newfoundlanders use a cast-iron pan) and cook on medium-low heat for about 20 minutes till the fat is rendered out. Using a slotted spoon, spoon the scrunchions into a small bowl, set aside and keep warm.

Add onions to sauté pan with the rendered pork fat. Cook on medium heat for about 20 - 25 minutes till browned and caramelized. You may need to add a little more oil or butter to prevent onions from burning. Set aside and keep warm.

While onions are caramelizing, drain watered salt cod and place in a pot, cover with cold water and bring to a boil. Reduce heat and simmer for 12 - 15 minutes. Remove cod to a large plate. Remove skin and bones from cod and discard. Set aside cod and keep warm.

Meanwhile add potatoes to pot and bring back to a boil. You only need enough water to barely cover potatoes. Reduce heat to medium and cook potatoes till almost cooked. Add hard tack. Continue to cook about 2 minutes. Drain and set aside. Keep warm.

Now bring everything together. In a large bowl, add the cod. Break apart cod keeping some bigger pieces. Add hard tack, breaking up the larger pieces. Add onions and any accumulated pork fat, potatoes and pork scrunchions. Add fresh ground black pepper to taste. Stir to bring everything together. Serve and enjoy.

Note: I use two full pounds of onions. I know it seems like a lot and it is but when caramelized they shrink a lot. So use them. On another note, I have no idea why you would, but some people cover their fish and brewis with molasses, others ketchup. I guess they just don't like the dish.

Pulled Pork Carolina-Style

You really need to try this recipe. It's really, really good. In the Carolinas, a BBQ is generally pulled pork, almost always served with a tangy, vinegar-based BBQ sauce. But that's where the similarities end because there is no single way to make a Carolina BBQ sauce. Eastern areas of the state tend to add mustard whereas the Western areas tend to add ketchup. I add a little of both to mine. Either way, there is a friendly rivalry as to which area of the state makes the best BBQ. And the version I created below is wonderful.

Serves 6 - 8

INGREDIENTS:

4 - 5 lb. bone-in pork shoulder
4 - 5 T dry rub (see page 256)

Rub the dry rub all over pork shoulder. Let sit overnight, refrigerated. Next day, smoke the shoulder 2 - 3 hours on low heat, about 200 - 250 degrees F. Feel free to omit the smoke. Just add another hour or so to the baking time.

Preheat oven to 250 degrees F.

Remove from smoker and put shoulder in a small Dutch oven. Add 1 cup of apple juice. Cover and bake for about 4 hours or until the meat shreds easily.

While the shoulder is cooking, make the vinegar sauce and set aside. Once the pork shoulder is cooked, remove from the oven. The shoulder should be falling-apart tender.

Spoon off any fat that might have accumulated in the pot. Discard any big chunks of fat, especially the flabby skin. Shred the pork in your pot, and add some of the vinegar-based BBQ sauce. Stir in BBQ sauce till all the pork is sauced. Serve on rolls of your choice with your favourite coleslaw.

CAROLINA VINEGAR-BASED BBQ SAUCE:

1 T olive oil
1 small onion, finely chopped
2 cloves garlic, finely chopped
1 ½ cups apple cider vinegar
¾ cup brown sugar, packed
¼ cup ketchup

2 T Worcestershire sauce
1 T dry mustard
1 t sea salt
1 t fresh ground black pepper
1 t red pepper flakes (or to your taste)

Heat a saucepan on medium heat. Add olive oil and sauté onions for about 6 - 7 minutes till onions are soft. Add garlic and cook for another minute or so. Add remaining ingredients and bring to a boil. Reduce heat and simmer for about 10 minutes. Remove from heat and stir into pulled pork.

Dry Rub

I created this dry rub, years ago, to use on baby back ribs. I had just come home from Cuba and brought back the finest ground coffee I had ever seen. So I decided to add it to my dry rub recipe. It adds another dimension to your barbecued food. Over the years I have used it on bone-in pieces of chicken, pork, chicken wings—anything you want to have good flavour when you are barbecuing.

Yields: about 3 cups

INGREDIENTS:

8 T sweet paprika

4 T smoked paprika

6 T fine sea salt

3 T fresh ground black pepper

1 t cayenne powder

2 T brown sugar

2 T white sugar

3 T garlic powder

6 T onion powder

4 T finely ground coffee

2 T thyme

2 T basil

2 T oregano

Mix all ingredients together. Store in a tight-fitting jar. Use it on ribs, chicken, pork or anything you want to BBQ.

If using it on pork ribs, remove the tough membrane on the back of the ribs. Place ribs meat-side down on a cutting board. Remove the membrane from the back of the ribs by gently inserting a butter knife between the bone and the membrane. Pick a bone in the middle of the rack. Be gentle and wiggle the knife. Get your finger between bone and membrane. Work your finger down the bone and eventually get a second finger in there. Pull membrane off and discard.

Rub a few tablespoons all over the ribs. Let sit overnight or if you are like me and do everything at the last minute, half hour before hitting the BBQ will work too. BBQ on indirect heat for about 2 - 3 hours until tender, then slather with your favourite BBQ sauce for the last 10 minutes of cooking.

BBQ Sauce

There really is no good reason to make your own BBQ sauce with all the flavours and styles available at the supermarkets, unless, of course, you want to make a better one than you can buy. Here is my version.

INGREDIENTS:

¼ cup olive oil
1 small onion, very finely chopped
2 cloves garlic, very finely chopped
1 cup red wine
1 cup ketchup
1 T fish sauce
2 T soy sauce

2 T sherry vinegar
2 T Dijon mustard
Dash of cayenne powder
1 t chili powder
2 T paprika
1 cup brown sugar
1 T liquid smoke

Heat a saucepan on medium heat. Add olive oil and sauté onion till soft, about 7 - 8 minutes. Add garlic and sauté for another minute or two. Add remaining ingredients to your saucepan. Bring to a simmer on medium heat.

Simmer for 10 minutes to bring all the flavours together. Let it cool and use as you would any BBQ sauce.

Foil-Wrapped Baby Potatoes

This dish works well on the BBQ while you are cooking your main course. Place the potatoes on the top rack away from direct heat. If you are cooking ribs or something that takes a long time, put your potatoes on the last 30 minutes of cooking time for your main.

Serves: 2
Preheat oven or BBQ: 300 degrees F

INGREDIENTS:

2 cups baby potatoes
8 - 10 small shallots, peeled and left whole
2 T chicken concentrate
1 t garlic powder
½ t dry thyme leaves

Dash of cayenne powder (optional)
Salt and fresh ground black pepper to taste
¼ cup white wine
⅛ cup water

Wash potatoes and cut in half. Put potatoes in a microwave safe dish and microwave on high for 4 minutes. Potatoes should still be a bit hard.

While peeling shallots, keep root end intact. It keeps them from falling apart. Add to potatoes and add remaining ingredients except the wine and the water. Stir to coat well.

Take a two-foot piece of foil wrap and fold in half. Place potato mixture in middle of foil and fold into a tight package, keeping one end open. Pour in the wine and water. Fold the foil in a tight pouch. Bake for 30 minutes in a preheated 300 degrees F oven or top rack of a BBQ till fork-tender.

Serve alongside your favourite BBQ dish.

Blackened Cajun Seasoning

Blackening food is a technique that is very much a part of the Cajun cuisine in Louisiana. Chef Paul Prudhomme created the blackened cooking method to try to capture the taste of fish or meat cooked directly over an open fire. Fish, chicken, pork and even beef take well to blackening. Generally, the food is dipped in melted butter and a blend of spices added before cooking. It's then placed in a very hot and dry cast-iron pan that has been heated almost to the smoking point. You should do this outdoors, as the moment your fish or chicken hits the hot pan, it smokes like hell. Chef Paul says the process creates an incredible amount of smoke, so much so that it will set off both your own smoke alarm and your neighbour's. If you haven't got the hint yet, cook this dish outdoors.

INGREDIENTS:

3 T paprika

1 T garlic powder

1 T onion powder

1 T dried thyme

1 t dried oregano

1 t cayenne powder (adjust to your liking)

2 t fine sea salt

1 t fresh ground black pepper

Mix all your spices together and store in a tight-fitting lidded jar.

TO BLACKEN YOUR FOOD:

Dip your meat or fish in melted butter, then shake a little seasoning on each side of your food. Place in your dry, very hot cast-iron pan.

Pour a tablespoon of butter atop each piece of meat or fish once you have it all in the pan. If you are using boneless skinless chicken breast or pork loin, pound them out to about ½-inch - ¾-inch thickness.

Cook no more than 4 - 5 minutes per side. If using shrimp, depending on their size, cook for only about 1 minute per side. If you have a heat gun, you want the pan at about 500 degrees before adding your meat or fish.

Cajun Corn (Maque Choux)

Summer vacation at the cottage is a well-loved tradition in Canada. I have the pleasure of enjoying cottage vacations at Big Bob Lake in Minden, Ontario. We always plan dinner as soon as we finish breakfast, and this normally includes a BBQ of some kind. It can be hard to find a side that everyone enjoys (outside of baked potatoes). One summer, I created my own version of maque choux, a popular Cajun dish. It was a real hit with the entire family and I continue to make this dish every summer for small family dinners and large parties. I particularly love it when the corn is freshly picked and purchased at a roadside stand heading up Highway 35 for a long weekend or to start a week's vacation.

Serves: 8 (stores well as leftovers for multiple meals)

INGREDIENTS:

6 ears of corn, shucked and kernels cut off
4 T butter
1 large Spanish onion, peeled
   and finely chopped
1 large clove garlic finely chopped
2 red bell peppers diced to ¼ inch

½ cup chicken stock
1 t smoked paprika
¼ t cayenne powder
1 t sea salt
½ t fresh ground black pepper

Heat a Dutch oven on medium heat. Melt butter and cook onion 5 - 6 minutes. Add garlic and cook for another minute or so. Add remaining ingredients including the corn, stir together. Cover and simmer on low heat for 10 minutes.

Serve as a side with your favourite BBQ dish.

Note: Feel free to roast the corn on your BBQ on high heat for a few minutes to get a little char on your corn.

Neapolitan-Style Pizza Dough

This pizza dough is made in the Neapolitan style. You have to use an Italian double-O flour, written as OO because it creates a perfect pizza dough. This recipe will yield enough dough to form about five medium-sized, thin-crust pizzas.

INGREDIENTS:

1 kg OO flour (about 8 cups)
1 T active dry yeast

30 g fine sea salt (2 T)
2 ½ cups warm water

Put flour in a mixer with the hook attachment in place. Turn mixer on low and add yeast and salt while mixing. Add water and mix for 8 - 10 minutes. Keep an eye on the dough as it has a tendency to climb up the hook. If it does, stop the mixer and push the dough back into bowl. After about 10 minutes of kneading, the bowl should be clean, and all the dough should be formed together around the hook.

Remove dough and place on a floured surface and knead for another minute or so. Form into a ball. Cover and let sit to rise until the dough has doubled in size. Depending on the temperature of the room, this will normally take about 2 hours.

Once it is has fully risen, portion dough into 5 equal-size pieces.* Form into balls by folding the dough up under itself using your fingers. If you plan to use the dough right away, cover and let rise until it doubled in size again.

This dough is best if made in advance and stored a day or two in the refrigerator. Remove from refrigerator 4 - 5 hours before you plan to use it to allow the dough to come to room temperature and rise till doubled in size.

Toss or roll out dough and use in your favourite pizza recipe.

* If you have a scale, each ball of dough should weigh approximately 330 grams.

Cheeseburger Pizza

Looking for ideas to make interesting pizzas, I decided to make my version of a cheeseburger pizza, cooked in my wood-fired pizza oven at 1000 degrees for less than 90 seconds. Stephen, a friend of mine, likes to add dill pickles to his burger and his pizza. I don't, I am a purist, so here you have nothing more than meat and cheese.

Makes: 2 pizzas
Preheat oven: 550 degrees on convection

INGREDIENTS:

2 portions of Neapolitan pizza
    dough (see page 264)
1½ lb. hamburger meat
1 t sea salt

½ t fresh ground black pepper
1 lb. old cheddar cheese
Ketchup
Yellow mustard

In a frying pan, add ground beef, salt and pepper. Cook on medium-high heat till meat is browned, about 7 - 8 minutes. Drain and discard any fat in the pan. Set aside.

Roll out pizza dough, or if you are adventurous, throw your dough in the air to get your dough ready. Sprinkle about a tablespoon of semolina on your peel and lay out dough on your peel or prepared pizza pan to about 8 inches - 9 inches in diameter.

Using a squirt bottle, add a nice layer of both ketchup and mustard. Then cover with half the ground beef and top with half the cheese. Now make your second pizza.

If you have a pizza stone, place in oven and heat to 550 degrees. Use your peel to transfer the pizza to your heated stone. Bake in a preheated oven for 8 - 10 minutes till crust is browned and cheese is melted. Enjoy.

Note: If you want the full hamburger experience, you can add some dill pickles, shredded lettuce and tomatoes after you remove your pizza from the oven.

Easy Frittata

This is my wife Gayle's recipe and it is so simple and delicious. She makes it for Sunday morning brunch or for when she's on a conference call while working from home. I love it with a side of bacon or blood sausage. Like most frittatas, you can really put anything in it, but my preference is onion, red pepper and mushrooms.

Serves: 2
Preheat oven: 375 degrees

INGREDIENTS:

2 T olive oil
1 medium onion, finely chopped
½ t garlic, finely chopped
½ sweet pepper, chopped
4 - 5 mushrooms, chopped
½ cup ham, chopped (optional)
4 large eggs

Pinch of cayenne pepper
½ t dry basil
½ t fish sauce (optional)
Salt and fresh ground black pepper to taste
½ cup Asiago cheese, grated
¼ cup Parmigiano-Reggiano or
     other hard cheese, grated

Whisk 4 large eggs in a medium bowl. Add cayenne, basil, fish sauce, Asiago cheese, salt and black pepper to taste. Set aside.

Heat a frying pan on medium heat and add oil, then onions. Cook for 3 - 4 minutes and add garlic. Cook for another minute. Add remaining vegetables and cook for 5 - 7 minutes. Add salt and black pepper to taste. Stir vegetable mixture and Asiago cheese into eggs.

Pour into a small greased baking dish. Top with Parmesan cheese.

Bake for 20 - 25 minutes in preheated oven. I tend to cook the first 20 minutes at 375 degrees and increase the temperature to 400 for the last 5 minutes.

Let stand for 2 or 3 minutes and serve.

Vegetable Jam

A few years ago, we were late planting our beets. That coupled with a not so good growing season, we ended up with a bunch of very tiny beets but the tops were wonderful. Always looking for something different and not wanting to waste these beet greens, I created this vegetable jam. It's probably not the right name as it's not sweet like a regular fruit jam, but it was delicious and goes well with a charcuterie board and for breakfast with eggs.

INGREDIENTS:

¼ cup olive oil

1 large onion, thinly sliced vertically (not crosswise)

5 large cloves garlic, coarsely chopped

1 lb. fresh spinach, chopped (or a bunch of baby beets and greens, chopped)

2 sweet peppers, cored and finely chopped

1 cup vegetable stock

½ cup white wine

½ t fish sauce (optional)

½ t *piment d'Espelette* (optional)

Salt and fresh ground black pepper to taste

Heat olive oil in a heavy-bottom pot on medium-high heat. Sauté onions till soft, about 10 minutes. Add garlic and sauté for a couple of minutes. Add remaining ingredients and simmer on low uncovered for about 20 minutes stirring occasionally.

Your vegetable jam should be thick like a fruit-based jam.

Serve with pork or any charcuterie board.

Homemade Aioli (Garlic Mayonnaise)

Aioli is a French term for a garlic mayonnaise. You can put a colourful spin on this classic French dressing, by adding a charred red pepper. Simply char the pepper, remove the charred skin and seeds and pulverize in a food processor or blender before adding to the aioli.

INGREDIENTS:

2 - 3 cloves garlic, very finely chopped

¼ t fine sea salt

3 egg yolks at room temperature

1 T lemon juice

1 T Dijon mustard

¼ t fresh ground black pepper

A couple good dashes of cayenne powder

¼ cup olive oil

¾ cup vegetable oil

Start by chopping the garlic very fine on your cutting board. Next, add your salt to the garlic and using the flat of your knife, drag the knife across your chopped garlic all while pushing the garlic into the board. This will help create a very fine mush.

Add garlic, eggs, lemon juice, mustard, pepper and cayenne to a bowl. Whisk to incorporate everything together. Mix the two oils together.

Slowly drizzle oil into egg mixture while whisking vigorously. As an alternative, you could use a handheld emulsion blender to bring it all together.

Store for up to 1 week in the refrigerator.

Food for a Crew

Lamb Stew for a Crew

I always loved making lamb stew with big meaty chunks of lamb, using a hind leg of lamb, which is more meaty and less fatty than the shoulder. But sometimes necessity is the mother of invention. One year, I was preparing for a big St. Patrick's Day party and wanted to make lamb stew. I was all out of lamb so I went to the supermarket to get a hind leg. I hit two or three stores, only to discover the only thing left was bone-in shoulder chops. I was not happy. They were frozen and very fatty but if I wanted a stew to celebrate Paddy's Day, I had no choice. Wow. What a difference the shoulder made. Now, I never use anything but shoulder to make a lamb stew. The flavour was nothing like I had ever made before. So my advice is, if you want a mediocre lamb stew, use the meaty hind leg. If you want a great stew, use the shoulder meat.

Serves: 20+ hungry mouths

INGREDIENTS:

5 lb. lamb shoulder cut into 1-in. cubes*
1 cup flour
2 T paprika
5 t salt
2 t fresh ground pepper
½ t cayenne powder
½ cup olive oil or as needed
2 - 3 lb. onions, peeled and chopped
4 cloves garlic, crushed
5 oz. can tomato paste

1 T fish sauce (optional)
3 litres lamb stock or Guinness or chicken stock or some combination thereof
7 large bay leaves
2 lb. carrots, peeled and chopped
1 large turnip, peeled and chopped
3 lb. potatoes, peeled and chopped
1 lb. parsnip, peeled and chopped
1 lb. fresh or frozen green peas
1 large ziplock bag

Add chopped vegetables in a bowl, cover with hot water. Set aside.

Add flour, paprika, salt, pepper and cayenne to a large ziplock bag. Shake. Add lamb and shake to cover.

Heat oil in heavy-bottom pot, sear lamb in batches till browned on all sides. Remove and set aside. Add onions and garlic, stir to brown for about 5 minutes. Add flour remaining in shaker bag to onions and stir till well mixed into the onions. Add tomato paste.

Stir and simmer for a few minutes. Add fish sauce, lamb, lamb stock and bay leaves, stir and simmer for about 45 minutes till lamb is somewhat tender.

Add chopped vegetables, and simmer till tender, about 40 minutes. Now add peas till warmed through. Remove and discard bay leaves.

Serve with crusty bread or rolls and enjoy.

*If you have to use the shoulder chops with the bone in, cut the meat from the bones but definitely add the bones to the stew. Remove them just before serving. They will add tremendous richness to the stew.

Beef and Barley Soup for a Crew

There is nothing like a big pot of soup. We often make one on the weekend, have a bowl for lunch and then separate it into one or two serving containers for future lunches. This particular recipe makes a nice-size pot of soup. Thankfully it freezes well.

Serves: 15 - 20

INGREDIENTS:

3 lb. beef, cut in small pieces
¼ cup olive oil
3 onions, peeled and finely chopped
2 cloves garlic, finely chopped
3 carrots, peeled and finely chopped
1 parsnip, peeled and finely chopped
1 small turnip, peeled and finely chopped
2 celery stalks, finely chopped

1 cup barley (pearl or pot, whatever you have)
12 cups good beef broth
5 bay leaves
¼ t cayenne
2 t salt
½ t fresh ground black pepper
2 t good soy sauce
1 t fish sauce

Cut beef into very small pieces, roughly ¼- inch cubes. Don't worry if they don't look the same. Keep in mind it's only a pot of soup. The goal is to have a nice variety of all your ingredients on each spoonful.

Heat oil on medium high in heavy-bottom pot. Brown beef cubes in batches ensuring not to overcrowd the pot. You want to brown, not steam the beef. After each batch, remove with slotted spoon and add next batch.

When the beef is all browned, add onions to the pot and sauté 5 - 6 minutes. Add the garlic and cook for another minute or so. Add the remaining ingredients including the beef to the pot.

Simmer for about an hour till barley is cooked. Remove bay leaves and discard. Taste and adjust seasoning.

Anise-Based Seafood Bisque for a Crew

Any time I brought my advisor team to my home for a business planning session, I served them this bisque. There were never any leftovers.

Serves 10 - 12

INGREDIENTS:

4 T olive oil
1 large Spanish onion, finely chopped
2 large carrots, peeled and diced small
3 cloves garlic, finely chopped
¼ cup butter
4 T flour
2 cups white wine
3 cups clam juice, seafood or chicken stock
1 small head fennel, finely chopped

2 (28 oz.) cans diced tomatoes
1 T dried dill or basil
7 bay leaves
1 T sea salt
1 t fresh ground black pepper
¼ t cayenne powder
5 lb. fresh seafood (scallops, shrimp, salmon, cod, halibut, etc.)

Heat a large, heavy bottom pot on medium-high heat. Add olive oil, chopped onion and carrot. Cook for 6 - 8 minutes till onions are soft. Add garlic and cook for another minute. Add butter and stir in the flour. When the flour is fully incorporated into the butter and onion mixture, add the wine and seafood stock. Bring to a simmer.

Now add remaining ingredients except the seafood. Cover and simmer for 20 minutes to allow the flavours to develop. Remove the bay leaves and discard.

Add the seafood and bring back to a simmer, about 10 - 15 minutes. Add the seafood in pieces as they will break up when you serve it.

Serve with crusty bread

Note: If you like saffron, this dish would be a great place to use it. Steep 1 gram of saffron in ½ cup of boiling water. Let sit for 20 minutes. Add to your pot when you add your stock.

Shepherd's Pie for a Crew

In my view, shepherd's pie can only be made with lamb. Use beef and you have a cottage pie. This shepherd's pie is a staple at my house for St. Patrick's Day. Served along with the lamb stew, you can comfortably fill your house for a Paddy's Day party and nobody will go home hungry.

I once had a bag of parsnips left over after making my stew, so I decided to add them to my mashed potato topping. It was a great addition. I will not make shepherd's pie ever again without using parsnips. Try it and your guests will agree.

Serves: 15 - 18
Preheat oven: 375 degrees

INGREDIENTS:

3 lb. ground lamb
2 lb. onions, peeled and finely chopped
2 large carrots, peeled and finely diced
2 T fresh garlic, finely chopped
3 T flour
¼ t cayenne pepper
2 t salt

½ t fresh ground black pepper
1 t good soy sauce
1 t fish sauce
1 cup Guinness or white wine
3 cups lamb stock (preferably) or chicken stock
3 cups fresh or frozen green peas

Heat heavy-bottom pot on medium-high heat. Brown the lamb, about 10 minutes. Add the onions, carrots and garlic and sauté an additional 5 minutes. Stir in the flour. Add the remaining ingredients except the peas. Simmer for 30 minutes stirring occasionally. Now add the green peas. Remove from heat and set aside.

While the base is cooking, it's time to make the topping.

TOPPING INGREDIENTS:

3 lb. potatoes, peeled and cut
    evenly into chunks
1 lb. parsnips, peeled and cut in thin disks

4 t salt
¼ lb. butter
½ cup lamb or chicken stock

Bring a pot of water to boil. Add the salt. Peel potatoes and parsnip. Depending on the size of the potatoes, cut into evenly-size pieces to cook all at the same time. Slice the parsnip into ¼-inch coins. This helps in the mashing process as the parsnip is very fibrous. Add potatoes to boiling water. Add parsnip about 5 minutes later.

Cook until both the potatoes and parsnip are tender. Drain and mash them together adding butter and stock to make smooth and creamy.

To prepare dish, spread the lamb base into 1 large casserole dish or 2 medium dishes. Top with potato, parsnip mixture. Spread evenly over the top. Bake for 35 minutes until it is bubbly and hot.

Grey Cup Chili for a Crew

There are probably a million recipes for chili out there. I like mine because it has a lot of ingredients that make a harmonious dish without any of the ingredients standing out. I like the texture of the cubes of meat and the addition of chocolate makes for a much richer chili. I sometimes omit the beans or add a Guinness in place of half the stock. Have fun with it.

Serves: 20

INGREDIENTS:

2 lb. beef, cut in ½-in. cubes

2 lb. pork shoulder, cut in ½-in. cubes

1 lb. ground beef

1 lb. ground pork

¼ cup olive oil

3 large onions, finely chopped

¼ cup fresh garlic, chopped

7 bay leaves

4 cups beef or pork stock

1 (28 oz.) can chopped tomatoes
    or 3 cups of chili sauce

1 T fish sauce

2 T sea salt

1 T fresh ground pepper

3 T oregano

8 T chili powder

2 T smoked paprika

2 (14 oz.) cans red kidney or pinto
    beans, drained and rinsed

3 oz. bittersweet or unsweetened dark
    chocolate (use cocoa powder if you
    don't have unsweetened chocolate)

3 - 4 green peppers, cored and
    diced into ¼-in. pieces

Brown all meats in small batches without overcrowding the pan. Remove each batch, trying to keep as much oil in pan as possible. Only add more oil if you need it to brown next batch. Reserve all cooked meats until all batches are cooked and set aside.

Add chopped onions and brown, 8 - 10 minutes. Add garlic and cook for just a minute or so.

Add the reserved cooked beef and pork, bay leaves, stock, fish sauce, tomatoes, salt, pepper and chili powder. (This is where your heat comes in by adding either mild or hot chili powder.) Bring to a rolling simmer, reduce to low, cover and simmer for 45 minutes until meat is tender.

Add kidney beans, chopped peppers and chocolate. Stir and simmer on low for another 15 minutes. Adjust seasoning.

Serve with garlic bread topped with cheddar cheese.

Baked Penne with Chicken, Peppers and Cheese for a Crew

If you are looking to make a dish for a crowd, this one will help. I cooked versions of this recipe as a fundraiser for our office a few times. Once I cooked it for International Women's Day and dyed the chicken purple. (You need about a 5:1 mix of red to blue to make purple dye.) I did a version of this for a St. Patrick's Day fundraiser, too. I'll leave it up to you to decide what colour to dye your chicken for St. Patrick's Day.

Serves 16 - 20
Preheat oven: 375 degrees

INGREDIENTS:

900 g penne pasta
¼ cup olive oil
4 lb. boneless skinless chicken thighs
3 t fine sea salt
1 t fresh ground black pepper

1 cup white wine or chicken stock
6 mixed sweet peppers
1 small Spanish onion, finely chopped
6 large cloves of garlic, finely chopped
2 lb. old cheddar cheese

Bring pasta to boil in salted water, simmer for 10 - 12 minutes until al dente. Drain and set aside.

Meanwhile, cut chicken thighs into 4 pieces. If using a dye, stir it in now. Heat a heavy-bottom pan on medium-high heat. Add a little olive oil to pan and sauté chicken in batches. Add the salt and fresh ground black pepper to chicken as you cook each batch. Remove chicken to a bowl. Set aside. Add white wine or stock and scrape all brown bits from the pan. Cook till reduced by half. Add to bowl with chicken.

Remove core from peppers and cut into roughly 1-inch pieces. Sauté peppers in a little olive oil for 3 - 4 minutes. Remove from pan and add to chicken. Add onion to pan adding a little olive oil if necessary and sauté for 3 - 4 minutes. Add garlic and sauté for another minute. Remove from pan and add to chicken and peppers. Stir the onions and garlic into the chicken and peppers.

Now bring everything together including the pasta in a large casserole dish. I use a large hotel pan big enough to hold it all. If you don't have one, you may need to use more than one casserole dish. Now cut the cheese into ½-inch cubes. Stir them into your dish.

Bake at 375 degrees for 35 minutes.

For the office, I would bake it in the morning before going to work. I then put the pan in a big chafing dish at the office to keep it warm.

Note: If you wish, you could add some mushrooms. I would add about 2 pounds cut in half and sautéed in butter for about 8 - 10 minutes. Add a little salt and fresh ground black pepper. You could swap the thighs for thinly-sliced chicken breasts if you wish.

Asian BBQ Ribs for a Crew

This recipe, along with a couple of sides, will easily feed 20 - 25 hungry mouths. To speed things up a little, bake these ribs in a covered roasting pan at 325 degrees for about two hours. This can be done a day in advance. Add two cups of boiling water to the pan, cover and bake. When ready to serve, grill on indirect heat for 30 - 40 minutes basting a few times.

Serves: 20
Preheat BBQ: 300 degrees F

INGREDIENTS:

10 racks baby back ribs or St. Louis style side ribs
3 cups hoisin sauce
1 ½ cup sauce
1 ¼ cup oyster sauce
1 ¼ cup soy sauce
1 ¼ cup honey
1 cup ginger, freshly grated

1 cup garlic, very finely chopped
½ cup sesame oil
½ cup Chinese Shaoxing wine or dry sherry
½ cup rice wine vinegar
1 T cayenne powder
5 T Chinese five spice powder
5 T orange zest

Mix all marinade ingredients together in a large bowl. Set aside.

Prepare the ribs for the marinade. You should remove the membrane to help the marinade penetrate the ribs. Place ribs meat-side down on a cutting board. Remove the membrane from the back of the ribs by gently inserting a butter knife between a bone and the membrane. Pick a bone in the middle. Be gentle and wiggle the knife. Get your finger between bone and the membrane. Work your finger down the bone and eventually get a second one in there. Pull membrane off. Discard. Cut ribs into 2 pieces.

Put prepared ribs in a large pan or a bunch of large bags. Add marinade and rub into the ribs. Let sit for a few hours or overnight in the refrigerator turning occasionally.

Remove ribs from pan or bags. Pour marinade into a large saucepan. Bring to a boil and turn off heat. Use to brush on ribs.

If you baked them already, you only need to give them another 30 - 60 minutes on indirect heat and baste often. If not baked, BBQ on indirect heat for approximately 2 ½ hours on a medium flame till tender. Baste occasionally.

Roasted Red Pepper Soup with Pears and Stilton for a Crew

I have been known to host some big events. This soup recipe will handily serve as a starter course for 50 - 60 people. Try to enlist some help roasting and peeling the peppers. It is also great to portion off and freeze as a basic roasted red pepper soup (without the pear or Stilton) for future dinners or lunches.

INGREDIENTS:

40 red peppers
¼ cup olive oil
1 ½ lb. butter
5 lb. onions, peeled and chopped
1 ½ cups flour
1 bottle white wine
12 litres chicken stock (about 48 cups)

3 T fish sauce
½ cup smoked paprika
3 T sea salt
1 t fresh ground black pepper
1 t cayenne powder
5 bottles of pears, drained and chopped
4 lb. Stilton, crumbled

To begin, rub whole red peppers with a little olive oil and roast over an open flame, high heat on a BBQ or under a broiler in oven, turning often until skin is completely black. Remove from heat and put peppers in a very large bowl, cover in plastic wrap and set aside for 20 - 30 minutes. This allows the peppers to cool and the steam helps the skin to come off easier. (Alternatively, use bottled roasted red peppers, rinsed very well.)

Meanwhile, sauté onions in butter for about 10 minutes in heavy-bottom stockpot on medium heat, stirring occasionally until onions have softened and started to brown. Add flour, paprika and cayenne to pot and cook for about two minutes stirring constantly without the flour browning. Slowly whisk in the wine followed by 1 cup of chicken stock.

When fully incorporated into the flour and onion mixture, stir in remaining stock and fish sauce. Bring to a light boil, reduce heat and simmer for approximately 10 minutes.

Remove all the black and blistered skin from the red peppers and be sure to remove the seeds and membranes from inside.

DO NOT wash the red peppers with water. Coarsely chop peppers. Add to stockpot along with any juices that has accumulated in the bowl and blend into a creamy soup using a hand held immersion blender.

Otherwise, working in small batches, add to a blender being careful of hot liquid, and blend to incorporate all ingredients into a smooth creamy soup. Continue to simmer for another 10 minutes or so. Don't worry if a few tiny bits of black skin stays on the peppers. After all, it's a fire-roasted red pepper soup.

Soup is now ready to be served or can be kept on a very low heat until ready to serve. Likewise, soup can be chilled and reheated on very low heat the next day, stirring occasionally.

To serve, pour about 1 cup of soup in each bowl, then add about ¼ cup of chopped pears to bowl, and top with some of the crumbled Stilton.

Dessert

Sticky Toffee Pudding

This is my take on this delicious English dessert. I recommend using large muffin tins for the best results on this recipe, and you absolutely need the sauce as it takes this dish to the next level.

Makes: approximately 12
Preheat oven: 350 degrees

INGREDIENTS:

1 ½ cups pitted dates, finely chopped (about 10 oz.)
1 ½ cups Guinness or strong coffee
1 ½ cups all-purpose flour
1 t baking powder
1 t baking soda
¼ t fine sea salt

½ cup unsalted butter at room temperature
1 cup dark brown sugar, packed
¼ cup white sugar
3 T molasses
2 t pure vanilla
2 large eggs, beaten
1 cup pecans, coarsely chopped

In a small saucepan, add the chopped dates and the Guinness (or coffee). Bring to a boil and reduce heat to a simmer. Continue cooking the dates until the Guinness is nearly all absorbed and the dates are soft, about 15 minutes. Turn off the heat and set aside.

Lightly butter and sugar (use white sugar) muffin tins. I used the larger style and had enough batter for 12 tins.

In a small bowl, sift the flour with the baking powder, baking soda and salt. In a larger bowl, or using a stand mixer, beat the butter with the brown and white sugars, molasses and vanilla until light and fluffy. Beat in the eggs, then fold in the pecans and dates and stir well. Now fold in the dry ingredients in batches till well incorporated.

Spoon the batter into the muffin tins and smooth the tops. I put just shy of half a cup of batter in each muffin tin. If you don't have enough batter to fill your 12 muffin tins, put a little water in the empty ones.

Bake for about 20 - 25 minutes, or until a toothpick inserted into the centres comes out clean. Although we are baking them in muffin tins, don't expect them to rise up out of the tins like muffins. When done, remove from oven. Remove from muffin tins and keep warm. Plate and serve with sticky toffee sauce.

STICKY TOFFEE SAUCE:

1 stick salted butter
1 ½ cup brown sugar, packed

1 cup heavy cream (35%)

In a medium saucepan, combine the butter, brown sugar and heavy cream. Stir over low heat until the sugar dissolves and the sauce is smooth and combined, 8 - 10 minutes.

Enjoy.

Old-Fashioned Bread Pudding with Vanilla Sauce

When we were growing up as children, we didn't have dessert very often but when we did, this was a staple and we sure enjoyed it. It's a great way to use up stale bread. My mother sometimes made a vanilla sauce to go with it. Yummy . . .

Preheat oven: 350 degrees

INGREDIENTS:

8 cups stale bread, cut in 1 - 2-in. cubes
6 large eggs, beaten
4 cups whole milk
1 ¼ cups brown sugar, packed
⅛ t fine sea salt
½ cup butter, melted

2 t nutmeg, fresh ground
2 T vanilla
½ cup chocolate chips or chocolate
  pieces broken up
½ cup chopped pecans

Butter a 3 - 4 quart casserole dish. Set aside.

In a large bowl add beaten eggs, milk, brown sugar, salt, melted butter, nutmeg and vanilla. Stir well. Add bread cubes and stir to help incorporate the milk mixture into the bread.

When almost all the milk mixture is soaked up by the bread, add the chocolate chips and the pecans. Stir once again and pour into prepared casserole dish. Bake for about 45 - 50 minutes till set in the middle.

VANILLA SAUCE:

½ cup unsalted butter
2 t flour
1 cup white sugar

½ cup heavy cream (35%)
1 T vanilla

Melt butter on medium heat in a saucepan. Add flour and stir till incorporated. Add sugar and cream.

Cook over medium heat, stirring occasionally until mixture thickens and comes to a boil, about 6 - 7 minutes. Remove from heat and stir in the vanilla.

Serve with bread pudding.

Carrot Cake

This is a classic dessert or treat for afternoon tea. It is a moist and rich version of carrot cake and one I hope you will add to your list of favourites.

Preheat oven: 350 degrees

INGREDIENTS:

2 cups flour
1 t cinnamon
½ t nutmeg, fresh grated
1 t mace
1 ½ t baking powder
¾ t baking soda
1 t fine sea salt
4 large eggs

2 cups brown sugar, packed
1 t vanilla
⅓ cup olive oil
⅔ cup corn oil
2 T orange juice
3 cups carrots, grated
1 cups pecans, chopped

Butter and flour a Bundt pan.

Sift together flour, cinnamon, nutmeg, mace, baking powder, baking soda and salt.

Beat together the eggs and sugar. Next stir in the vanilla, oils and orange juice. Then add the dry ingredients to the wet ingredients in batches stirring until incorporated.

Stir in the carrots and pecans.

Pour into prepared pan and bake for 50 - 55 minutes. A toothpick inserted in the centre should come out clean. Let sit in pan for 5 - 10 minutes. Then turn out on a rack to cool. Ice with cream cheese frosting when cooled.

CREAM CHEESE FROSTING:

8 oz. cream cheese at room temperature
2 T whipping cream (35%)
1 t vanilla

2 cups icing sugar
Pinch of fine sea salt

Beat cream cheese and whipping cream together. Add vanilla and slowly beat in the icing sugar and salt on slowest setting until smooth.

Lemon Pound Cake
(My Wedding Cake)

Those of you who know me, know I'm not known for my baking skills. However, when Gayle and I got married, I couldn't resist baking our wedding cake. My sister Shirley decorated it. Here is the recipe, reduced to a more manageable, Bundt pan size.

Preheat oven: 350 degrees

INGREDIENTS:

3 cups flour
1 t baking powder
½ t fine sea salt
1 cup unsalted butter
1 ⅔ cups white sugar
⅓ cup light brown sugar

4 eggs, separated
1 cup buttermilk
1 t pure vanilla
2 T lemon zest
2 T lemon juice

Butter and sugar a Bundt pan.

Sift flour, baking powder, and salt together in a bowl. Using an electric mixer, cream together the butter and sugar until light and fluffy. Gradually beat in eggs, one at a time, into the butter mixture. Then add vanilla, lemon zest and lemon juice. Gradually add the flour mixture and the buttermilk to the butter mixture.

Pour into prepared Bundt pan. Tap your Bundt pan a few times on a double layer of a tea towel on your counter to settle the cake mix. Bake for 60 - 65 minutes until a toothpick comes out clean. Turn cake out on a rack while still warm.

If you wish, you can glaze the cake with this syrup.

SYRUP INGREDIENTS:

¼ cup water
¼ cup white sugar

2 T fresh lemon juice

Combine the water and sugar in a saucepan and bring to a boil. Remove from the heat and stir in the lemon juice.

Place a paper towel under the rack to catch the drippings of the syrup. Gradually brush the hot syrup over the warm cake, taking your time to let the syrup soak in.

Cherry Pound Cake

This is a simple cake to pull together. Don't forget to add a little flour to your cherries. If not, they will all sink to the bottom of your cake.

Preheat oven: 325 degrees

INGREDIENTS:

1 cup salted butter at room temperature
1 cup white sugar
4 large eggs, beaten
1 t lemon or almond extract
1 t vanilla

2 cups flour plus 1 T
½ t baking powder
¼ cup cherry juice
¾ cup halved maraschino
    cherries, well-drained

In a large bowl, or using a stand mixer, cream together the butter and sugar. Add beaten eggs one at a time and then add the lemon or almond extract and the vanilla.

Add a tablespoon of flour to the halved cherries to cover them. Don't skip this step. It ensures the cherries won't all sink to the bottom of the pan.

Then add the baking powder to the flour and stir into the flour. Now stir in the flour, cherries and juice to the creamed mixture. Stir till well incorporated.

Pour the cake batter into a buttered and floured loaf pan.

Bake for 70 minutes. Check for doneness by inserting a toothpick into centre of cake. Toothpick should come out clean. If there is cake on toothpick, bake for an additional 10 minutes.

Turn cake out of pan to cool on a rack.

Partridgeberry and Orange Cake

Partridgeberry season begins in Newfoundland after the first frost. So, my sister Shirley went picking them, right when I was preparing this cookbook for printing. When she got back home, she texted to tell me she had picked over a gallon and I should include a recipe for them in my cookbook. So I took my cherry pound cake recipe, made a few changes and here you have it: a partridgeberry and orange cake.

Preheat oven: 325 degrees

INGREDIENTS:

1 cup salted butter, room temperature
1 ¼ cups white sugar
4 large eggs, beaten
1 cup Greek yogurt
1 T orange extract
Zest of 2 large oranges

1 t vanilla
2 cups flour plus 2 T to dredge
   the partridgeberries
2 t baking powder
2 cups fresh or frozen partridgeberries

Stir in 2 tablespoons of flour to the partridgeberries. Don't skip this step. It ensures the berries won't all sink to the bottom of the pan.

Remove the zest from the oranges by carefully peeling the oranges with a sharp knife. Try not to remove the white pith, just the outer zest. Cut the slices of zest into small thin strips.

In a large bowl, or in a stand mixer using the paddle attachment, cream together the butter and sugar. Add beaten eggs one at a time and then add the yogurt, orange extract and vanilla.

Next, add the baking powder and the orange zest to the flour and stir in. Now stir in the flour into the creamed butter mixture, till just incorporated. Gently fold in the partridgeberries, being careful not to burst the berries.

Pour the cake batter into a buttered and floured Bundt pan. Tap your pan a few times on a folded over tea towel on your counter to settle the cake mix.

Bake for 50 - 55 minutes. Check for doneness by inserting a toothpick into centre of cake. Toothpick should come out clean. If there is cake on toothpick, bake for an additional 10 minutes. Turn cake out of pan to cool on a rack.

If you wish, you can glaze the cake with this syrup.

SYRUP INGREDIENTS:

¼ cup water
¼ cup white sugar

2 T orange extract

Combine the water and sugar in a saucepan and bring to a boil. Remove from the heat and stir in the orange extract.

Place a paper towel under the rack to catch the drippings of the syrup. Gradually brush the hot syrup over the warm cake, taking your time to let the syrup soak in.

A Soldier's Christmas Pudding

My best friend, Kevin, was a big military buff. He did so much for the Newfoundland Regiment that he was eventually appointed Honorary Colonel of the Regiment. One night early in December 2002, we were having dinner and thinking about what we could do to celebrate his appointment. It was about the time I would be making my Christmas puddings. We thought, how about making Christmas puddings and sending them overseas to our Canadian soldiers who were stationed in Afghanistan? We met with the Armed Forces Station Commander, Gary Reddy. He thought it was a great idea and he got approval from his superiors. The only command we were given was that the puddings had to be alcohol free. We sent enough Christmas puddings for our 500 troops on Christmas Day that year.

We didn't stop there. For the next seven years, while our Canadian troops were stationed overseas, we sent them Christmas puddings. Each year the numbers got higher until, in the final year, we made Christmas puddings for 5,000 soldiers. Kevin, his wife Dale and I, with some occasional help, brought it all together every year for the eight years our soldiers were stationed in Afghanistan, and we called ourselves "the pudding people from Newfoundland."

Here is the recipe cut down to a very much more manageable size. As you can imagine, this recipe easily doubles, triples, quadruples . . .

And here's to our Canadian men and women who serve our country.

Makes: five 28 oz. tomato can–size puddings

INGREDIENTS:

1 ½ cups ground beef suet (room temperature)
½ cup unsalted butter (room temperature)
1 ½ cups light brown sugar
2 eggs, beaten
2 T corn syrup
3 cups mixed red and green
    candied cherries (whole)
2 cups mixed peel
1 cup sultanas
1 cup golden raisins
1 cup currants
½ cup candied pineapple, chopped
2 cups white all-purpose flour

1 cup breadcrumbs
¼ t cinnamon
¼ t allspice
1 t mace
1 t salt
1 cup pecans, coarsely chopped
1 cup blue potatoes, grated
1 cup carrots, grated
½ cup parsnip, grated
1 cup buttermilk or milk mixed
    with a little vinegar
1 t baking soda
½ cup white grape juice or brandy if you wish

Use white granulated sugar and melted butter to prepare tins.

Brush five 28 oz. cans with melted butter and shake with granulated white sugar. Cut 5 disks of parchment paper slightly smaller than the size of the can. Place in the bottom of each prepared can. Set aside till ready to fill. Have a double layer of tin foil and butcher's twine ready to seal cans.

Blend suet (partially melted) with the butter, brown sugar and corn syrup. Beat eggs in a separate bowl and add to suet mixture. Set aside. This should be the largest bowl, as all other ingredients will be added to this one.

Measure out all fruit and pecans in a bowl. Pour white grape juice over fruit and let sit till ready to use. In another bowl, sift dry ingredients, flour, breadcrumbs, spices and salt together. Just before adding fruit mixture to batter, add a little of the dry ingredients to the fruit and stir. This is a necessary step as it helps keep the fruit suspended in the pudding.

In another mixing bowl, grate potatoes, carrots and parsnips.

In a large measuring cup or bowl, measure out buttermilk and add baking soda, mix. (Note: if baking soda is good, the buttermilk should foam.) Set aside.

Now it's time to bring everything together. Start by adding the dry ingredients to the suet and butter mixture. Mix well. Add half of potato carrot and parsnip mixture, half of the fruit mixture and half the buttermilk; mix well. Add the balance of the ingredients and mix well.

Spoon the batter into your prepared cans till they are approximately ¾ full. If you have a scale, your can and pudding should weigh approximately 750 grams. Shake down or tap on a solid surface a couple of times to fill any air pockets. Cover with double layer of foil and tie tightly with a double layer of butcher's twine. Place in a pot with a rack and cover to two-thirds with boiling water.

Bring back to boil and reduce heat to medium low for approximately 3 ½ hours. You want to ensure you have a light rolling bubble to your water. Keep an eye to water levels and add boiling water when necessary. Your pudding is done when top does not appear shiny. The best way to test for doneness is to insert a toothpick. If it comes out clean it's done, if not steam for another 15 minutes.

When done, remove from pot, and remove foil. Let pudding sit in can for 5 — 10 minutes, then turn over on a rack and remove can. Remove and discard parchment paper. Let dry overnight and then wrap in plastic wrap.

Pudding can be stored in refrigerator for a week, if not freeze. To reheat, wrap in foil and heat in a warm oven for 30 minutes.

Serve with the delicious rum or bourbon sauce on page 303.

Note: Many of my friends have intentionally frozen their puddings, and tell me it's even better the following year.

Rum Sauce for Christmas Pudding

If you are as fortunate as I am, the holiday season is filled with memorable moments, friends, family and an abundance of food that includes those special recipes that only get served during this festive time. Christmas pudding is a rich, dense desert that is very traditional fare in Newfoundland to enjoy after a big turkey dinner. What makes the pudding truly enjoyable is the rum sauce. This is my version and I hope it becomes part of your holiday tradition as it has for me.

INGREDIENTS:

1 cup water
¾ cup brown sugar
¼ t vanilla

4 t cornstarch
½ cup rum*
1 T butter

In a small saucepan, bring water to boil with the brown sugar. Blend cornstarch with a small amount of water and slowly add to sugar mixture. Stir continuously.

When thickened, add vanilla and rum and barely bring to a boil. Remove from heat, whip in butter and serve with your Christmas pudding. If you desire a thinner sauce use less cornstarch.

Hint: Flambé pudding with ¼ cup of warmed rum before serving.

*Replace rum with bourbon or 1 teaspoon of rum flavouring

My Mother's Boiled Blueberry Pudding

Every Sunday, my mother cooked a big dinner for our family of 13, served midday, around 12:30 or 1:00. This meal always included a big boiler of salt beef and vegetables, a roast of some sort baked in the oven with gravy and her infamous boiled pudding.

This pudding was made with fresh blueberries or raisins, and sometimes she'd add molasses. Once the pudding was mixed, she'd spoon it into a pudding bag, made from a heavy cheesecloth-type of material, tie the top with a piece of string leaving a little head space for the pudding to rise. Then, she'd lower the filled bag into its own boiler of boiling water. I remember she'd always put a plate in the boiler to prevent the pudding from scorching. We had it on our dinner plate with the gravy on top, but it also can be served as dessert with ice cream.

INGREDIENTS:

2 cups flour	2 eggs
4 t baking powder	¾ cup milk
¼ t salt	1 t vanilla
½ cup sugar	1 cup blueberries
¼ cup butter	

Use a medium-size pudding bag (about 6 inches square). Mix together all dry ingredients. Cut in butter. Beat eggs, add milk and vanilla. Add to the dry mixture. Fold in blueberries, or you could use raisins, figs or other berries instead.

Spoon into pudding bag and tie the bag tight with string, leaving about 1 inch of head space for the pudding to rise.

Fill a pot to about ¾ full with water, and bring to a boil. Put a plate in bottom of boiler and lower pudding into boiler. Simmer for 1 ½ hours. Remove pudding from boiler. Gradually ease the bag off the pudding and put into an uncovered casserole or serving dish, and place in warm oven for 10 - 15 minutes to let the pudding dry out a bit.

Serve with dinner or as a dessert with vanilla ice cream.

Tea Buns

This recipe should make approximately two dozen tea buns depending on the size you cut them. Somewhere between two-and-a-half and three inches is a good size.

Preheat oven: 400 degrees

INGREDIENTS:

4 cups all-purpose flour
1 cup butter
8 t baking powder
½ cup sugar
½ t salt

1 cup whole milk
½ t vanilla
2 eggs beaten
½ cup raisins (soak in 1 cup hot
water for 10 - 15 minutes)

In a large bowl, mix dry ingredients together. Cut in butter using a pastry cutter until butter pieces are pea-size. Mix wet ingredients and add to dry ingredients. Drain raisins and add to mixture. Fold together to form a soft dough.

Move dough to a floured surface. Fold together. Don't overwork the dough. It will develop the gluten and the buns will be tough. Fold over a maximum of 10 - 12 times. Flatten or roll dough out to about ½-inch thick. Cut out tea buns using a circular cutter or a water glass.

Place buns on parchment lined cookie sheet touching each other. Bake 12 - 15 minutes till browned nicely and almost doubled in size.

Note: Replace raisins with chopped candied ginger for a refreshing change. Do not soak the ginger in water. Just cut into small pieces.

Galette

A galette is a free-form French pastry. It's so much easier than making a pie because it's very rustic and hard to mess up. Use almost any firm fruit like apples, peaches, plums, pears, etc.

Preheat oven: 400 degrees

INGREDIENTS FOR THE PASTRY:

1 cup flour, plus a little additional
flour for the board
2 t baking powder
Pinch of salt
½ cup white sugar

1 stick cold butter, chopped
1 egg, beaten
⅓ cup cold whole milk
1 t vanilla

FOR THE FRUIT:

3 cups mixed firm fruits
¼ cup brown sugar
1 T flour

1 t fresh grated nutmeg
1 T lemon juice

FOR THE EGG WASH:

1 egg, beaten
⅛ cup coarse Demerara sugar or raw sugar

FOR THE PASTRY:

The key to a good tender pastry is handling it as little as possible. Start by sifting flour, baking powder, salt and sugar together in a bowl. Chop butter in pea-size pieces. Rub into flour. Add milk and vanilla to beaten egg and add to dry ingredients. Barely mix the pastry and refrigerate your while you prepare your fruit.

FOR THE FRUIT:

Peel your fruit and cut into thin slices. Add sugar, flour and nutmeg to a bowl stir to incorporate. Now add the fruit slices and lemon juice. Stir to bring everything together. Set aside till pastry is ready.

Lay out a large piece of parchment paper. Lightly dust paper with flour. Dump your barely-mixed pastry on flour lined parchment paper. Fold together pastry folding no more than 12 times.

Using a rolling pin (or empty wine bottle, like I do), roll out your pastry to about ⅛ inch in a rough circle shape. Don't worry about the exact shape. That's the beauty of a galette. No matter if it's round or oval, it will still taste good. Now using the parchment paper, lift your pastry to a cookie sheet.

Now let's bring this galette together. Spoon out fruit mixture in centre of your pastry to within 2 - 2.5 inches of the edge, leaving any juice behind. Start folding edges up over your fruit. Gently pinch where the edges overlap. Continue all the way around your galette till all edges are rolled in.

FOR THE EGG WASH:
Brush edges with egg wash and sprinkle the Demerara sugar on the egg wash.

Bake in preheated oven for about 25 minutes till browned. Remove from oven. Let cool a little and serve with vanilla ice cream.

Agnew's Chocolate Terrine

This is a very decadent dessert. A little goes a long way. This is my boss, Dave's, favourite dessert. Any time we cooked a dinner together or I organized a dinner where he was present, he would ask me to make this dessert and would often insist that everyone at the table try some. So, I'm including this recipe for him. Here's to you, Dave, and the many meals, bottles of wine and dessert we have enjoyed together.

Serves: 10 - 12

INGREDIENTS:

700 ml heavy cream (35%)
1 ½ lb. milk chocolate
¾ lb. dark chocolate

4 large egg yolks
2 ½ sticks salted butter at room temperature
3 T cognac

Heat cream in a double boiler. If you don't have a double boiler, a regular heavy-bottom pot will suffice; however, don't leave it on the stove unattended. The moment you walk away it will boil over. Bring to a boil. Add chocolate and stir till melted. Remove from heat. Stir in egg yolks. Then add butter and stir till incorporated. Stir in cognac.

Line a terrine or a loaf pan with plastic wrap. Pour in the chocolate mixture. Tap on a dishcloth on counter to help settle and then smooth top. Chill till set or overnight.

Next day, invert terrine on a board. Remove plastic wrap. Using a warm knife cut into ½-inch slices. Serve with Newfoundland bakeapple jam or a strawberry or raspberry sauce.

BERRY SAUCE:

1 lb. strawberries or raspberries
4 T icing sugar

1 T lemon juice

Mash berries in a bowl. Push through a strainer to remove the seeds. Add icing sugar and lemon juice. Mix well. Spoon atop chocolate terrine. Top with a little whipped cream if you desire. Enjoy.

Chocolate Fudge Rum Cake

If you are looking for a dense, chocolaty fudge cake, this one's for you. I was aiming for a Caribbean chocolate rum cake but ended up with this fudge cake. C'est la vie!

Preheat oven: 350 degrees
Butter and sugar a Bundt pan

INGREDIENTS:

3 cups flour
¾ cup dark cocoa powder
1 t baking powder
½ t fine sea salt
1 cup unsalted butter
1 ⅔ cup white sugar

⅓ cup light brown sugar
3 oz. dark chocolate, melted
4 large eggs
1 cup sour cream
1 t pure vanilla
¾ cup black rum

Sift flour, cocoa powder, baking powder, and salt together in a bowl. In the bowl of an electric mixer, cream together the butter and sugar until light and fluffy. Add melted chocolate and beat till incorporated. Gradually beat in eggs, one at a time, into the chocolate butter mixture. Then add vanilla and rum. Gradually add the flour mixture and the sour cream to the butter mixture.

Pour into prepared Bundt pan. Bake for 65 - 70 minutes until a toothpick inserted into the centre comes out clean.

Once cake is baked, remove from oven and set on a baking rack; do not remove cake from Bundt pan.

FOR THE RUM GLAZE:

½ cup butter
¼ cup brown sugar

¾ cup black rum

Melt butter and sugar in a saucepan. Add rum and barely warm the rum.

Brush the rum glaze over the warm cake. It is best to do this when cake is still warm so rum can absorb into the cake. Brush the rum glaze until the cake has absorbed all the glaze. This may take a while. Save a little of the glaze to brush on the cake after you remove it from the Bundt pan.

Completely cool the cake for 1 - 2 hours in the fridge before taking it out of the Bundt pan. You want the glaze to set completely inside the cake. Turn the cake out on a cooling rack. Use wet, hot dish cloths around the Bundt pan to help release the cake from the pan. Brush with the remaining glaze.

Light Fruit Cake

If you are going to bake one cake, why not bake four or five?
Same effort, five times the results.

Preheat oven: 250 degrees F using convection heat

INGREDIENTS:

½ cup white sugar
1 cup water
1 T corn syrup (clear)
1 cup brandy or white rum
3 cups white seedless raisins
3 cups red cherries, chopped
3 cups green cherries, chopped
½ cup dried candied lemon
1 cup dried candied orange
2 ½ cups dried citron

2 ¾ cups candied pineapple, chopped
¾ cup chopped candied ginger, chopped
3 cups sliced almonds
4 cups pecan halves
8 eggs, beaten
2 cups butter
2 ½ cups sugar
4 cups flour
1 t baking powder
1 T mace

Make a syrup by boiling water and sugar together. Then add the corn syrup. Remove from heat.

Mix all the fruit and nuts together in a large bowl. Stir in the syrup and the brandy, then soak overnight.

Prepare four 9-inch x 5-inch loaf pans. Butter the pans and line with parchment paper.

Now it's time to prepare the batter. Cream butter and sugar well. Beat eggs and gradually beat into the sugared mixture.

Sift together flour, baking powder and mace.

Add the dry mixture to the batter and barely stir the two mixtures together. Then add the prepared fruit. Mix with your hands.

Spoon into prepared pans and bake for 3 - 3 ½ hours at 250 degrees convection heat until a cake tester comes out clean.

Note: If your fruit has dried out like mine has, add an extra ½ cup of brandy to soak them overnight.

Dark Fruit Cake

This was a very popular cake in Newfoundland households at Christmas time in yesteryears. Sadly, it's becoming a lost art these days.

Preheat oven: 250 degrees F

INGREDIENTS:

3 cups mixed candied peel
5 cups raisins
2 cups red candied cherries, halved
2 cups green candied cherries, halved
2 cups chopped pecans
1 ¼ cups dark rum
1 cup butter
2 ½ cups dark brown sugar
¾ cup cooking molasses
5 large eggs

1 T vanilla
½ cup orange juice
3 ½ cups flour
1 t baking powder
½ t salt
2 t cinnamon
1 t nutmeg
1 t allspice
1 t ground cloves

Combine fruit and nuts in a large bowl. Pour the rum over the fruit and marinate for 24 hours or overnight. Stir often. Butter and line one large round cake pan (9-inch springform pan at least 3 inches deep) and two loaf pans with parchment paper or brown paper.

Preheat oven to 250 degrees F on convection heat.

Drain the rum from the fruit and reserve. Add ½ cup of flour to the fruit. This is a necessary step as it helps keep the fruit suspended in the cake. Mix thoroughly.

Cream butter, sugar and molasses together. Add eggs one at a time and continue beating. Stir in the vanilla, the reserved rum liquid and the orange juice.

Add the baking powder and the spices to the flour. Stir to combine. Add dry ingredients in batches to egg mixture and stir to combine. Now add to the fruit mixture. Using your hands, fold everything together.

Turn into prepared pans, smoothing out the top and using convection heat, bake for 3 hours or until a cake tester comes out clean.

When cakes are cooled, you can brush the top and sides with a little black rum. The more times you brush the cake, the more flavour you will develop. Let age 2 - 3 weeks before cutting.

Chocolate Rugelach

These chocolate rugelach are one of my favourite cookies. They are difficult to find so you will have to make your own. They come from the Jewish populace of Poland.

Yields: approximately 48 pieces

INGREDIENTS FOR THE CREAM CHEESE DOUGH:

2 ½ cups flour, plus a little more for your board to roll out your dough
½ cups white sugar
1 T mace (or 1 t cinnamon if you prefer)

1 (8 oz.) package cold cream cheese, cut into cubes
1 cup or 2 sticks cold salted butter, cut into cubes

FOR THE CHOCOLATE FILLING:

10 oz. good quality dark or semisweet chocolate, finely chopped
½ cup apricot jam

2 large egg yolks
⅓ cup coarse sugar like Demerara or raw sugar

Make the dough by combining the flour, sugar and mace together. Then add the cream cheese, butter, flour and sugar mixture into the bowl of a food processor. Pulverize the ingredients until the cream cheese and the butter are mixed into the flour and begin to form into a ball.

Remove the dough from the food processor, squeezing it into a ball, then wrap with plastic wrap and refrigerate for at least an hour.

Remove your dough from the refrigerator after your hour has elapsed, and cut dough into four pieces. Let it rest for about 10 minutes before you start to roll it out.

Lightly flour your work surface, then using a rolling pin, roll out one of your four pieces of dough into a circle about ⅛-inch thick.

Now brush the rolled-out dough with one-quarter of the the apricot jam and then sprinkle one-quarter of the finely chopped chocolate pieces onto the dough, pressing lightly into the dough.

Cut the dough into 12 wedges. Roll each wedge up, starting from the wide end, then twist to form a crescent shape. Repeat for the other 11 pieces.

Now do the same for the other three pieces of dough.

Place each rugelach on a parchment paper-lined baking sheet, keeping space between each one, and refrigerate for about 30 minutes. (You can also freeze some of the rugelach and bake later.)

Preheat the oven to 350 degrees.

Brush the tops of the rugelach with the egg wash then sprinkle them with a little of the Demerara sugar.

Bake for 18 to 20 minutes or until golden brown. Transfer to a cooling rack to cool. Enjoy.

Sauternes-Poached Pears

*Sauternes is a French sweet wine from the Sauternais region of the Graves
section in Bordeaux. It can be expensive, so if you don't want to use a Sauternes,
try using white grape juice, a white port or another sweet wine like a Zinfandel.
This is a lovely light desert that is wonderful to enjoy all year round.*

Serves: 8

INGREDIENTS:

4 Bosc pears, peeled
375 ml Sauternes
1 cup water
½ cup white sugar
Pinch of salt

6 T mascarpone cheese at room temperature
3 T Stilton or other blue cheese
   at room temperature
Whipped cream (optional)

In a saucepan just big enough to fit the 4 pears, bring the Sauternes, water, sugar and the salt to a light simmer. Add pears and poach till tender. Remove pears from saucepan and reserve poaching liquid. Chill pears. After pears have chilled, cut in half lengthwise. Remove the core.

While pears are poaching, blend mascarpone and Stilton together. Place a knob of the mascarpone–Stilton cheese mixture in the centre of the pear, where the core was removed. Set aside.

Reduce poaching liquid to a heavy syrup.

Place pear cut side down on a plate. Drizzle some of the reduced poaching liquid over the pear, allowing some to decorate your plate as well. Add some whipped cream if you wish.

Note: This dish would be kicked up a notch if you made a chocolate ganache and used it to decorate your plate even more. Make chocolate ganache with both sweet and bittersweet chocolate and heavy cream. Pipe into a bag and drizzle over pear. You can even pipe a strip to look like the pear stalk.